A WEAVER'S TALE

The Life & Times of the Laxey Woollen Industry
1860-2010

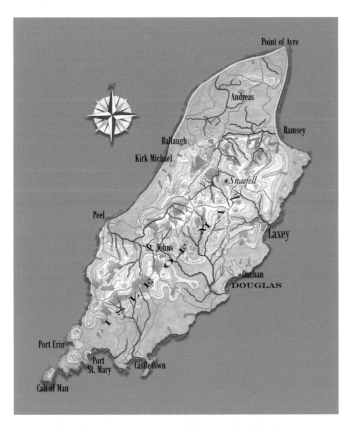

The Isle of Man is one of the British Isles. It is a self-governing nation located in the middle of the Irish Sea between Scotland, England, Ireland and Wales. Laxey is a village on the east coast of the Island in the parish, or district, of Lonan

Sue King

First published in softback in 2010 by St George's Woollen Mills Ltd.
Glen Road
Laxey
Isle of Man
IM4 7AR
www.laxeywoollenmills.com
For more information e-mail: info@laxeywoollenmills.com

Produced and printed by Mannin Media
Media House
Cronkbourne
Douglas
Isle of Man

Author: Sue King
Designer: Julia Ashby Smyth
Typeset by Steve Moore, Mannin Media

ISBN: 978-0-9564553-1-4

CONTENTS ✺

The colour coding for each chapter is a light-hearted reference to the predominant clothing shades of the various eras...

Extract from

'The Noble Art of Weaving'

A Poem by James Maxwell

Of all the arts that Minerva taught,
None ever were to such perfection brought
As that of weaving. This all arts excels;

And let us ne'er forget. This art was giv'n,
By free donation of indulgent heav'n;
For when mankind was made in innocence,
No clothes were needful then for his defence.
But when man fin'd 'twas granted him to wear,
Clothes to defend him both from flame and air.
Then let us not hereof attempt to boast,
Since clothes are only marks of glory lost;
But let us still adore the gift of heav'n,
That for our comfort this grand art was giv'n.

Let every trade extol the Weaver's name,
By whom is rais'd, their honour, wealth and fame
Yea, let them be esteemed and lov'd by all,
By whom supported are, both great and small.

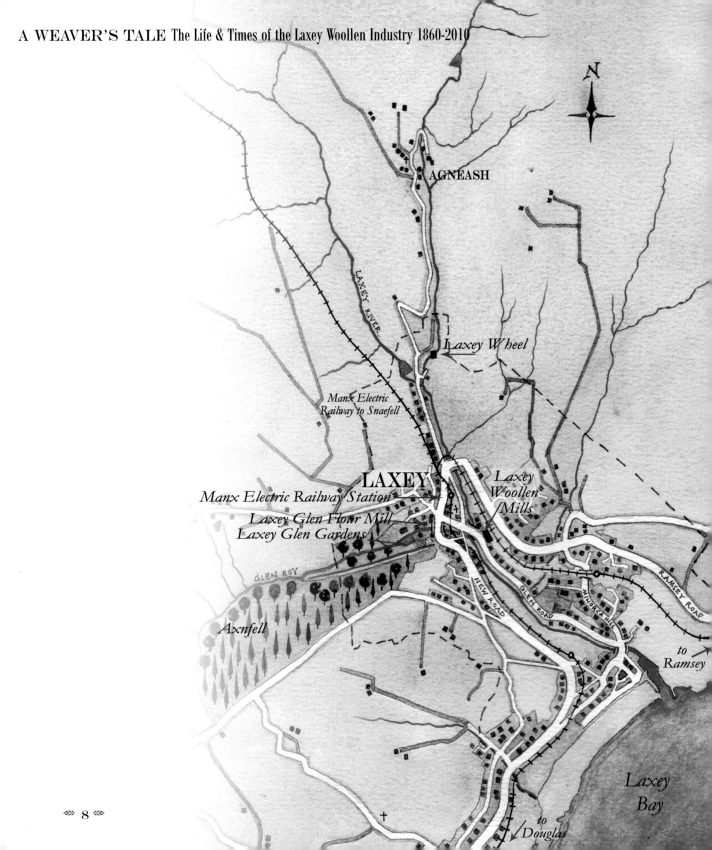

AGNEASH

LAXEY RIVER

Laxey Wheel

Manx Electric
Railway to Snaefell

LAXEY

Manx Electric Railway Station

Laxey Glen Flour Mill
Laxey Glen Gardens

Laxey
Woollen
Mills

GLEN ROY

Axnfell

NEW ROAD

GLEN ROAD

MINORCA HILL

RAMSEY ROAD

to
Ramsey

Laxey
Bay

to
Douglas

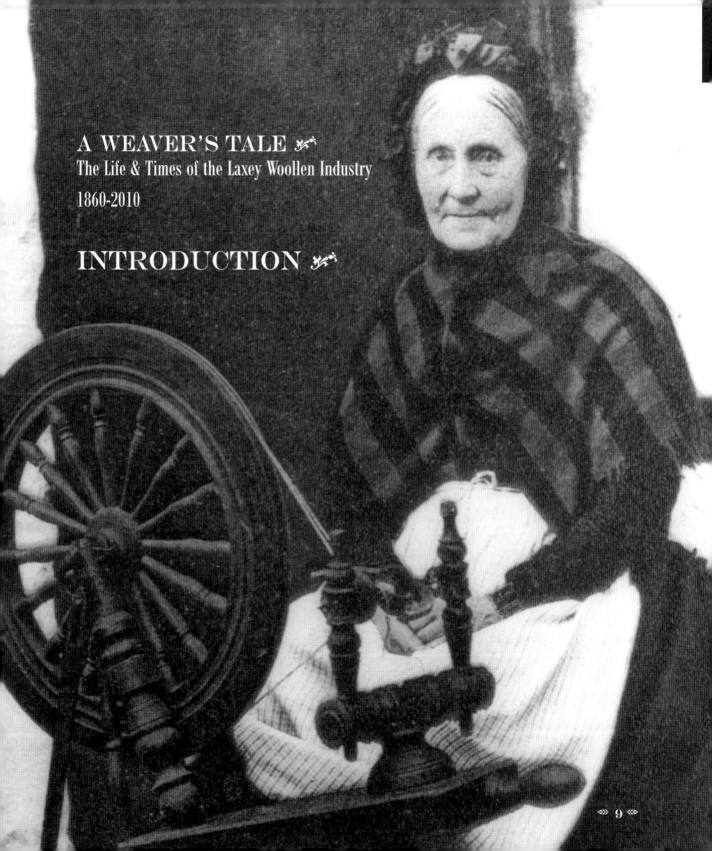

A WEAVER'S TALE ✺

The Life & Times of the Laxey Woollen Industry

1860-2010

INTRODUCTION ✺

INTRODUCTION

Wool has been relied upon by mankind for warmth and comfort for at least 12,000 years. In Biblical times it is even said to have helped assuage thirst - a woollen fleece left out overnight to gather dew would be wrung out in the morning to provide water. But its main function throughout history has been for clothing. As long ago as the Iron Age, man in Britain was using sheep shears and making rudimentary woven fabric. In the Isle

of Man, ninth century Viking settlers brought their weaving skills with them and used the wool from native sheep to make thick, warm, cloaks and tunics. Yet, despite being one of the oldest textiles known to man, wool has never been truly replicated. Quite simply, it is one of the most extraordinary natural fibres there is.

What makes wool so distinctive? Well, it has a number of unusual characteristics which give it a definite 'edge'. Firstly, it has an almost magical ability to deal effectively with both cold and warm conditions. In cold situations the air trapped between its fibres acts as insulation, keeping the wearer warm, but in warm situations this same process allows the wearer to keep cool by allowing air to cool the body[1]. Wool also has the ability to absorb moisture yet still feel relatively dry – a quality exploited by farmers and fishermen for centuries. Woollen fibres have a highly absorbent core and a scaly surface which is water repellent. This allows perspiration or water to be drawn away from the body, preventing clammy skin.

The structure of wool also makes it flame resistant, meaning it will smoulder rather than burn when it overheats – hence the old advice to smother chip pan fires with a woollen blanket! It's also incredibly strong. A single woollen fibre can be bent 20,000 times without breaking. This is because it is made from a complex protein called keratin, the same matter that makes human nails and hair[2].

All of these intriguing properties have been put to good use since man first learnt to gather wool but they've also given it added status as an indicator of security, comfort and social standing.

Did you know?

The world's oldest, existing woollen carpet was made in the Fifth century BC. It was discovered inside the frozen tomb of a nomadic tribal chief in Southern Siberia. Even though it was made two and a half thousand years ago the design and colours are still worthy of any modern home-furnishing store

Woollen cloth has been manufactured in Britain for hundreds of years but it wasn't until the Middle Ages that it began to play a central role in the country's economy. This was prompted largely by the migration to England of Huguenot weavers fleeing persecution in France and Belgium. The Huguenots were renowned for their textile skills and were encouraged in their trade by the English monarchy. The subsequent growth of the cloth industry led to greater numbers of sheep being bred and before long every country in Europe was relying on England for their wool supplies.

To encourage the manufacture of woollen cloth statutes were introduced, such as the requirement of the dead to be buried in wool. British wool exports became subject to tax and even the simple nursery rhyme 'Baa Baa Black Sheep' has been interpreted as a political satire on the wool revenue gained by King Edward I in 1275 ('one for my Master'). By the time King Edward III came along wool was being employed in the highest circles in the land – red wool cushions were introduced into the English Parliament and even today, in the House of Lords, the Lord Chancellor still sits upon the Royal Woolsack to address the peers of the realm.

In the middle of the eighteenth century woollen cloth was Britain's most important product, with manufacturing extending from the Scottish Isles to East Anglia. But it was still essentially a 'domestic industry' in which the raw wool was spun into yarn on a cottage spinning wheel then woven into cloth on a cottage loom. This, however, was not to last. Before long the Industrial Revolution took wool from the home to the factory and by the mid nineteenth century the British wool industry was employing two hundred thousand people[3]. But while large scale manufacturing introduced regular wages and constant work it also brought smoke, pollution, overcrowded housing, oppression and long working hours. Children could begin work in woollen factories as young as five years of age and many working class people found themselves enduring terrible social conditions. Even the idea of a 'working class' was a new phenomenon – people who no longer worked by their own clocks but were forced to obey the rules of a factory and the commands of a mill master or overseer. The contrast to the quiet routine of home spinning and weaving couldn't have been more marked.

Setting The Scene

Important developments in Laxey prior to 1860

1800-60	Reverend Fitzsimmons began planting up the Victoria Park
1825	Primitive Methodist Church built near the harbour (now a nursery)
1834	National School built just below the Ramsey Road
1835	All Saints Church, Lonan, consecrated
1836	The Laxey Glen Infant School opened at the bottom of Church Hill
1841	Lonan population 2,230
1846	The Glen Methodist Chapel built (now Palladian House)
1851	Lonan population increased to 2,607
1854	New Road bridge completed
1854	The opening of the Laxey Wheel, attended by nearly 4,000 people
1856	Christ Church consecrated. Built on land donated by George Dumbell and constructed by his mining company

"Manx Sun" Series. 183

The Starting of the Great Water Wheel, Laxey, Sept. 1854. From an Old Print.

Early Manx Weavers

The earliest physical evidence of Manx weaving dates back to Viking times. The wool was spun into threads using hand spindles, then arranged vertically and weighted down by perforated stones. In a process known as 'drop weaving' horizontal threads were interwoven through the vertical threads and this was repeated until a cloth was produced.

As time went on wool was increasingly seen as a valuable commodity. By the sixteenth century Manx law forbade the export of wool and fines were applied to anyone who transgressed. In 1511 William McStoile of Lonan was fined 'two shillings for sailing with wool beyond the country, contrary to the order of the Lord and his council'[4]. This ban on wool exports existed right up to the nineteenth century and all raw material and finished cloth was destined for the home markets only.

In the seventeenth century the Lord of Man, James, Earl of Derby brought artisans over from England to teach cloth-making skills and before long spinners and weavers in every Island sheading were being encouraged in their craft, with generous monetary prizes awarded for their handiwork[5]. Somewhat shockingly, misdemeanours involving wool could quite literally be a matter of life or death. If you were caught clipping another person's sheep and the value of the wool was less than sixpence you would be physically punished, but if the value was more than sixpence you would be sentenced to death![6]

There were a number of different sheep breeds on the Island but the most important was the native Loaghtan, a small, hardy breed with soft wool that varies from light to dark brown, depending on how much sunlight it is exposed to. The very name Loaghtan roughly translates as 'mouse-brown'. The wool is not only hard-wearing and good for spinning and weaving but has the distinct natural advantage that it doesn't need dyeing. Tailors favoured it for making men's suits, waistcoats and trousers and it made very warm, long socks known as stockings.

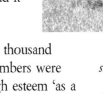

A fine Manx Loaghtan sheep. The wool on his back fades naturally in the sun

Loaghtans are thought to have existed on the Isle of Man for over a thousand years, possibly originating from Scandinavia[7]. Unfortunately their numbers were never very big and clothing made of Loaghtan wool was held in high esteem 'as a sort of national distinction'[8].

By the late eighteenth century every district of the Island had at least one woollen weaver, known in Manx as 'fidder'. Most rural Islanders were crofters, eking out a living from their own crops and animals, so it made sense for their clothes to be produced within a radius of just a few miles. Weavers were generally known by their occupation eg. Juan-y-fidder or John the Weaver, and they were usually adept at weaving in both wool and flax, producing clothing, blankets, felt hats, quilts and stockings. Wool was also used for decorative home furnishings, tapestry and embroidery.

In the early nineteenth century farmers were given permission to import sheep from England and within fifty years the number of sheep on the Island had trebled [9]. However, not everyone saw this as a good move. Thomas Quayle wrote that 'much mischief has been, and still is, done to the quality of Manks wool by the importation many years ago of a Scotch breed called the Linton, the wool of which is coarse and neither fit for combing or carding' [10]. Other sheep bred on the Island in the mid-nineteenth century included Ryeland Merinos, Southdowns, Leicesters and Scottish black face sheep. Some of these were cross-bred with Loaghtans and the most successful in terms of wool was Merino-Loaghtan which was sought after for its softness and could be made up into fine, blue-dyed cloth [11].

At around this time the relaxation of stringent duties and licences on wool production also encouraged the setting up of small woollen mills all over the Island, where cloth could be produced in commercial quantities.

But despite this introduction of mechanisation the production of woollen cloth in the Isle of Man remained a largely cottage industry until the mid-nineteenth century.

Machinery

'Machinery was erected for the spinning, dressing and dyeing of the native wool and for its manufacture into cloth for home consumption. To the farmer this has been highly beneficial by creating a steady market for his wool and the cloth of this fabric is of good quality. Dispersed through the country are several small bleach-fields, fulling mills, dyeing houses etc. at which these domestic manufactures are completed.'
('General View of Agriculture in the Isle of Man' by Thomas Quayle, 1812)

Hand loom weaver James Creer of Colby. Similar scenes were once common in Laxey

Weaving in the home was traditionally done by men and spinning by women.

The business of spinning and weaving at home had a lot going for it, especially the ability of whole families to work together, doing away with the need for childcare. A woman could card and spin wool while pregnant or nursing young babies and her older children could work alongside her, helping with simple tasks. Weavers usually required the services of more than one spinner which made spinning a sought-after skill and the sooner children could learn it the sooner they could add to the family's income. The working conditions in the home, as compared to a factory, were also relatively healthy with the opportunity to work outdoors in warmer weather and indoors in the winter. Other chores could be fitted in around the spinning work. If a woman was widowed or unsupported, spinning was a useful trade to know as it avoided the need to work away from the home.

Weavers

'Weavers were plentiful in those days (the 1840s). Our blankets, flannels, cloth for the men's suits, plaids for us women's frocks or dresses, all made at home, spun by mother with a woman to help.'
(Life in Ballaugh in the 1840s by Ellie Shimmin)

Unfortunately the very term 'cottage industry' has come to imply a quaint simplicity that is somewhat misleading. Romanticised images showing bonneted women spinning in front of neat, thatched cottages while the man of the house quietly sucks on a clay pipe, have fed a perception of domestic textile workers as simple, uneducated country folk. In fact, weaving was by no means confined to rural areas. Many weavers active in the Isle of Man in the first half of the nineteenth century were actually living and working in Douglas in the area of Cattle-Market Street (now Market Street) and Bigwell Street (now upper Lord Street).

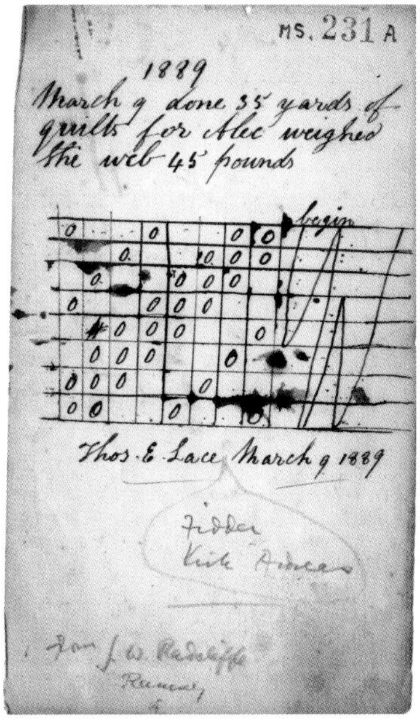
MS. 231 A
1889
March 9 done 35 yards of quilts for Alec weighed the web 45 pounds
Thos. E. Lace March 9 1889

The notebook of Andreas hand loom weaver Thomas Lace. The sketch is for cloth with a diagonal design

Home spinners and weavers also had to be intelligent and organised. Wool spinning requires great care and skill, and domestic weavers were really 'small businessmen' who almost certainly had to know how to read and write. Not only did they need to set up, work and maintain a hand loom – a complicated piece of equipment by any standard – but they needed to keep orders, organise raw materials, design patterns and weigh and measure fabric. The notebook of Thomas Lace of Andreas provides a rare, enlightening glimpse into the daily life of a working Manx hand loom weaver in the nineteenth century. Within this tiny book are detailed drawings of patterns; notes such as 'done 35 yards of quilts for Alec, weighed the web 45 pounds'[12] and a record of sheep shearing dates – all hints as to the complexity of a weaver's daily business.

Laxey Weavers

In the Laxey area, domestic hand loom weavers were scattered throughout the valley, from the bottom of Old Laxey Hill to hillsides in the shadow of Snaefell mountain. In the early part of the nineteenth century the district was home to an astonishing 22 hand loom weavers[13], many of whom wove both wool and flax – the latter to make linen - but by 1851 this number was reduced to 12 and by 1861 it had halved again to just six. Growing competition from English, Continental and Manx mill-manufactured woollen cloth no doubt made business tough for the home weaver, but it was the success of the Laxey Mines that was probably the main contributor to their demise – by 1860 most young men were opting to earn greater money by going down the mines rather than following their fathers into the weaving trade.

The cottages occupied by Laxey's weavers would have been quite distinctive. Natural light was vital to their craft so the dwellings were usually built with larger than normal front windows. In rural areas these buildings were usually single-storeyed and the wooden loom was either kept in the main cottage, which must have made life pretty cramped, or in a small stone building attached to the side of the house

A rare surviving example of a weaver's shed (Cregneash)

known as a 'weaver's shed'. Spinning would be done in the parlour during the winter and outside during the summer. Ideally the cottage would also have some open land facing the sun on which washed new cloth could be dried on wooden frames called 'tenters'.

One of the few remaining cottages to be identified as an early Laxey weaver's cottage lies ruined in eerie isolation on a steep hillside known as the Lhergy Veg or Little Slope, opposite Agneash. The property dates back to at least the 1870s[14] and although the dwelling itself is small it appears to have had a weaver's shed alongside and a number of outhouses. Above and below are steep, sunny aspects perfect for wind-drying new lengths of cloth.

The ruins of a weaver's cottage at Lhergy Veg in the Upper Laxey Valley lie just below the Mountain Railway embankment

Life in this remote upper corner of Laxey valley must have been undeniably tough. The only way in and out of the property is miles of steep, rough track and the effort required to bring sacks of raw wool to the cottage and take woven cloth to the fulling

mill would have been incredibly arduous. The nearby fields were said to be 'infested with fairies'[15] and it's easy to believe it. Fairies, good or bad, may at times have been the only company for the family living there.

But although this particular example of a weaver's cottage paints a lonely picture, it's unlikely that Laxey's textile weavers ever worked in total isolation as they relied on a number of other tradesmen for equipment and tools. The blacksmith was an essential ally, providing the wire for carding combs, metal tenter hooks for suspending damp cloth, and making and sharpening metal shears and clippers.

The services of a local joiner or carpenter were necessary for crafting the hand loom and wooden tenter frames. The manufacture of loom shuttles, spinner's chairs and oak spinning wheels was a craft in itself and this was the job of the wood turner. Then there were the wool sacks, wool weights, dyeing vats, writing paper and implements for designing patterns and keeping orders, weighing and measuring instruments; in fact a plethora of large and small items needed to run what was essentially a 'small business'.

The weaver may also have had animals and a few crops to supplement his weaving income and cultivated plants to help with the cloth manufacturing process. The giant spiky heads of teasel were ideal for carding or teasing the wool and an assortment of plants were available from which to obtain natural dyes.

A Weaver's Year

Common Teasel *'Leaddan'*

A typical annual cycle for a Laxey home-based woollen weaver began with the shearing of the mountain sheep which usually took place at the end of the winter and again in late summer. The fleeces would then be bundled up in large sacks and taken to the weaver's cottage where the women and children would pick out any grass, dung, briars and dirt and wash the wool with water and soapwort. Soapwort is a garden plant that contains chemicals called saponins which, when agitated with water, create a foamy lather. The washing helped to remove excess grease known as lanolin, although a small amount was usually retained to make spinning easier.

The clean wool was then combed or carded, either with dried teasel heads or pairs of small wooden paddles studded with short spikes of metal wire. This straightened the fibres and made them lie parallel, ready for spinning. Carding can be a lengthy business, however, and by the early nineteenth century the process was often carried out away from the home in purpose-built carding mills. Robert Corlett ran a successful carding mill alongside his dye-house and spinning mill on the banks of the river in Laxey Glen (now called Glen Road)[16]. Here the wool was passed over giant, spiked rollers then bundled into rolls ready to be spun at home.

Spinning wheels have been in use for over five hundred years but early models were very basic and it wasn't until the addition of treadles that they became properly efficient. Rhythmically depressing the treadle with the foot causes the

> **Did you know?**
> *Lanolin is secreted by the sheep's sebaceous glands. It is used in many modern cosmetics as it is easily absorbed by the skin.*

spinning wheel to rotate and carded wool is gently guided with the fingers onto the wheel where it is twisted into yarn. The yarn is then carefully removed and wound into hanks, ready for dyeing or weaving.

If the finished cloth was to feature a multi-coloured pattern the spun yarn would be dyed at home before weaving, but if it was to be used for single-coloured blankets or plain flannel the cloth would be dyed after weaving, usually in a commercial dye-house. Home dyers grew many plants, and gathered seaweeds and berries, from which to extract a range of colours such as blue (woad plant), red (madder plant), yellow (weld plant) and green (dullish seaweed). The plants were gathered in the summer and hung from the rafters of the house to dry.

Yarns dyed with natural dyes such as plant extracts, berries and vegetable skins

Learning to spin and weave started at an early age, with children simply watching parents plying their craft and later being given the chance to 'have a go' before possibly taking up a proper apprenticeship. Weaving requires great patience, concentration, nimble fingers and keen eyesight. Winter was the weavers' busiest time and they often had to work by artificial light. Prior to the introduction to the Island of cheap paraffin oil in 1870[17] weaving families relied on candlelight or dip lights, made by dipping the pith of a rush in a mixture of boiling tallow and beeswax. Empty scallop shells could also be filled with wax and a wick and made into rudimentary but effective candles.

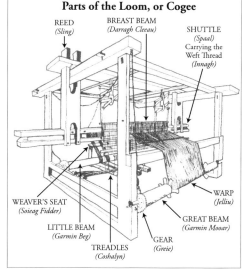

Parts of the Loom, or Cogee

REED
(Sling)

BREAST BEAM
(Darragh Cleeau)

SHUTTLE
(Spaal)
Carrying the
Weft Thread
(Innagh)

WEAVER'S SEAT
(Soieag Fidder)

WARP
(Jelliu)

LITTLE BEAM
(Garmin Beg)

GREAT BEAM
(Garmin Mooar)

TREADLES
(Coshalyn)

GEAR
(Greie)

Plying a hand loom for hours a day is hard, physical work using both the arms and the legs and but weavers were paid according to a system called 'yarding'[18] earning one halfpenny for each yard of blanket cloth they produced, so obviously more hours meant more money. By spring though, the cloth was usually ready for the next stage of the process and the weaver could take a break from his loom and turn to fishing and crop growing to subsidise his income.

When the cloth came off the loom it was coarse and loose, similar in texture and appearance to sack-cloth. Some cloth was worn in this 'unfulled' state but it was generally taken to a fulling mill, also known as a walk or tuck mill, where it was tightened, strengthened and waterproofed. Fulling usually took place in the summer months so it was important for the mill to be close to a full flowing river or stream, accessed by green tracks and near to a ford or bridge. Laxey has had fulling mills for at least five hundred years – the Manorial Roll of 1511-15 refers to two 'waulk' mills in the area[19] and by the early nineteenth century Southward & Corlett had established the Laxey Tuck Mill on the banks of the Laxey river halfway down Glen Road[20].

The cloth was taken from the weaver's house to the fulling mill by horse and cart where it would be placed in a wooden trough filled with water and degreasing agents and pounded vigorously for about six hours. This forced the tiny scales on the woollen fibres to mesh together, tightening and softening the cloth. In early times the cloth was literally 'walked' by men and women with bare feet (not a pleasant job!) but by the nineteenth century it was done by large wooden 'stocks' – pairs of giant, water-powered hammers which alternately rose and fell on the wet cloth, beating and turning it. Fulling required great skill as the operator of the stocks had to judge exactly the right amount of time and pressure applied. If the cloth wasn't beaten enough it would have a loose texture, but too much and it would over-shrink – or end up full of holes. When the stocks were in 'full swing' the noise would be heard for miles around. Manx folklore even makes mention of fairies being driven out their homes by the noise and vibration from the fulling mills!

The pounding was divided into three sessions[21]. The first involved water and stale urine, collected from local households, and the second session involved water and fuller's earth, a glacial deposit extracted from the ground as a fine clay and dried into powder[22]. Intriguingly, Laxey tuck mills had a Manx source for their fuller's earth in the nineteenth century as it was mined on the Island's west coast at Cooil Dharry in Upper Glen Wyllin. The final session of pounding was carried out in hot water mixed with a natural detergent like soapwort, followed by thorough rinsing.

After fulling, white blankets and the tawny-brown woollen cloth made from the native Loaghtan wool were left in their undyed state, but cloth to be coloured was treated by a professional dyer. Southward & Corlett operated dyeworks alongside their fulling mills and most dyers would collect cloth or wool for dyeing from outside the district as well. As early as 1802 Laxey dyer Thomas Brownrigg was travelling into Douglas on a regular basis and accepting customers outside 'The Sign of the Windmill' tavern [23]. Here customers would place their wool or cloth in a sack marked by a wooden tally indicating their colour preference and the following week the dyed product would be brought back to the same meeting place and claimed by the tally on the sack [24].

Once the cloth was fulled or dyed it had to be carefully dried and, as this was usually a summertime procedure, this was done outside the weaver's house on wooden tenter frames (from the Latin 'tendere' meaning 'to stretch'). The edges, or selvedges, of the damp cloth were hooked on to small metal hooks called tenterhooks running along a high wooden bar, then the cloth was pulled tightly downwards and the opposite edges were attached to a bottom parallel bar. The tenter frames were positioned to catch as much wind as possible and once fully dried the cloth was taken down and gently brushed with dried teasels to raise a soft, downy nap, then carefully trimmed with large shears to produce a smooth surface.

The finished cloth was then ready for the arrival of the local tailor who would make it up into suits, jackets, caps, skirts and waistcoats. More straightforward items such as blankets, flannel underwear, shawls and woollen petticoats would be sewn up by the woman of the house. Quantities of spun yarn were also kept aside for the knitting of stockings, loose-weave shawls, jumpers and baby clothes.

A section of old tenter frame, studded with metal tenterhooks

The Demise of Cottage Industry

By 1860 domestic cloth manufacture in Laxey was on the decline, many of the processes were being carried out away from the home and the core skills of spinning and weaving were losing favour. Technological innovations that improved the weaver's output could still be used in the home – namely John Kay's flying shuttle and Hargreaves' spinning jenny – but it was the new inventions that were simply too big to fit in a cottage that spelt the death knell for the home-based hand loom weaver. Richard Arkwright had already patented the water frame – a machine for spinning yarn, Samuel Crompton invented the mechanised 'spinning mule' and, most crucial of all, Edmund Cartwright invented a power loom which replaced hand workers with a machine.

All of these new inventions could be driven with power generated by water wheels and the landscape of the Isle of Man was perfect for such development. An abundance of hills, valleys, fast-flowing rivers and streams and high rainfall meant water mills were almost guaranteed success. With carding, dyeing and fulling taking place away from the home by the early nineteenth century the scene was set for weaving and spinning to follow suit.

References:
1. 'The Fabric of History' by Nina Hyde, National Geographic Vol. 173 No.5 May 1988
2. ibid
3. 'Expansion, Trade and Industry' John Child, Heinneman 1992
4. Lonan Manorial Roll 1511, Oxford University Press 1924, reprinted in A Manx Notebook, ed. Frances Coakley
5. 'The Manx Woollen Industry Through the Ages' J.W. Cowley lecture to IoMNHAS, reprinted Ramsey Courier 27th Dec. 1957, p.41
6. 'Historical and Statistical Account of the Isle of Man' Ch.XVII, Joseph Train, Quiggin, Douglas 1845
7. J.W. Cowley, ibid p.40
8. 'General View of Agriculture in the Isle of Man' Thomas Quayle, Bulmer & Co., London 1812, reproduced by MHF 1992 p.112
9. 'Tholtans of the Manx Crofter' G. Kniveton & M. Goldie, The Manx Experience p.13
10. Thomas Quayle, ibid p.112
11. Quayle, ibid p.113
12. Notebook of Thomas Lace, Andreas weaver MS 231A, MNH
13. 1841 Lonan census, MNH
14. 1869 Ordnance Survey map, Lonan
15. 'A Manx Scrapbook' No.1, W.W. Gill, Arrowsmith 1929 p.279
16. Manx Sun 10th July 1852, MNH
17. G. Kniveton & M. Goldie ibid
18. J.W. Cowley ibid p.44
19. Lonan Manorial Roll 1511, ibid
20. Manx Advertiser 6th December 1831, MNH
21. St John's Mill information leaflet 2009
22. British Geological Survey, Mineral Fact Sheet
23. Manx Advertiser 8th May 1802, MNH
24. 'Colour from the Countryside' Mona Douglas, Manx Star 19th March 1973, MNH

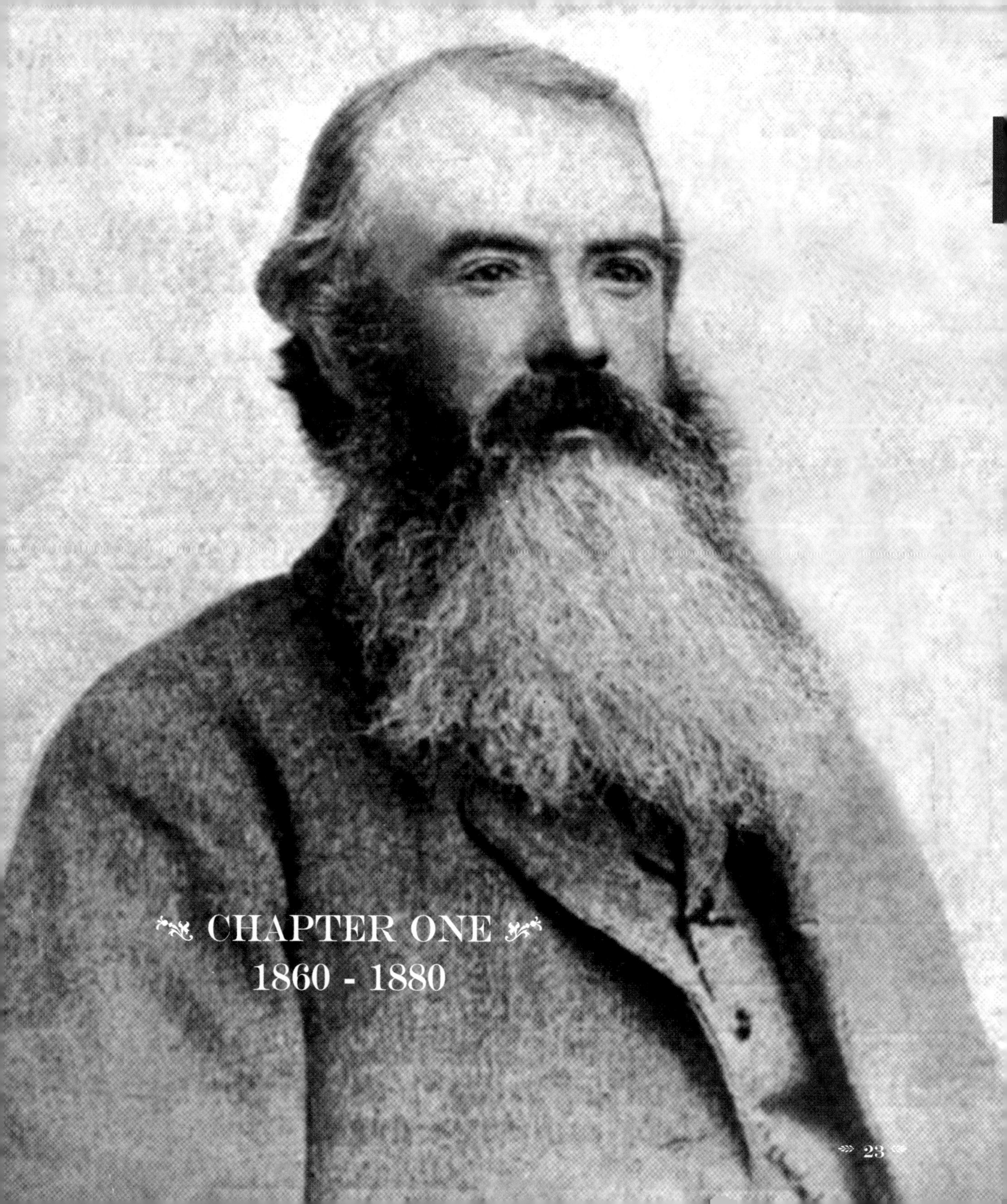

CHAPTER ONE
1860 - 1880

Timeline

1860	Laxey Flour Mill founded by Captain Richard Rowe
1861	The Warehouse on the quay built as a grain store by Captain Rowe
1861-69	Dumbell's Terrace built to house miners
1862	Formation of The Great Laxey Mining Company
1867	Formation of the 'Sons of Mona' Rechabites
1868	The National School built on Ramsey Road
1868	Development of Victoria Park by Robert Williamson
1870	Severe winter. Laxey Wheel completely frozen by heavy ice
1870	Minorca Primitive Methodist Chapel constructed
1870	Laxey Industrial & Provident Co-operative Society established
1870-80	New distinction between Old and New Laxey in official registers
1870-80	Mining for lead, zinc, silver and copper in Laxey at its peak
1871	The Great Snaefell Mining Company established
1871	Fatal stabbing at the Bridge Inn after a fight involving two miners
1871	Old Laxey Reading Room established (now the sailing club)
1872	The Old Laxey Equitable Co-operative Society opened at the bottom of Minorca Hill
1872	Great strike at Laxey mines
1873	The Laxey Steamship Company started up
1874	New school built at South Cape under the Manx Education Act
1874	Loss of steamer 'Blende' en route from Laxey to Swansea. 7 lives lost
1877	Nearly 14,000 people visited the Laxey Wheel
1877	Working Men's Institute opened in New Laxey
1877	Opening of Ballagawne elementary school
1877	Major outbreak of smallpox forced the closure of Laxey schools
1879	A second lengthy strike at the Laxey mines

Laxey Life

Cast your mind back to the mid-nineteenth century and it's tempting to imagine the small seaside village of Laxey as a rustic hamlet populated solely by miners and farmers. But at a time when other parts of the Island were shrinking in population Laxey was visibly expanding year on year and many of its residents were forward-thinking Victorian businessmen whose energy transformed the village. By 1860 a steady influx of English and Irish workers had boosted the population to around three thousand and new schools and churches were springing up to support the increasing number of families. Local industry included dyeing, paper-making, wool carding, flour milling, cloth fulling and flax processing and, alongside mining and farming, many individuals found work as shoemakers, teachers, bakers, butchers, dressmakers, gardeners, tailors, blacksmiths, corn millers and export agents.

New settlers weren't, however, the only people keen to taste what Laxey had to offer. By the 1860s thousands of British workers, keen to escape the pollution and overcrowding of the industrialised northwest, were spending their precious holidays in the Isle of Man and many enjoyed a day trip to Laxey by horse and carriage or passenger steamer. Those wishing to stay longer could also enjoy comfortable accommodation at the Queens or Commercial hotels.

The beach had no formal promenade but a number of miners owned fishing boats which they hired out to day trippers and the water was considered good for bathing. Up in New Laxey visitors could spend many relaxing hours in the tree-lined gardens of Victoria Park, later developed with tearooms and recreational areas as the Glen Gardens. They could also visit the district's prosperous mineworks which were as much a tourist attraction as a heavy industry. As early as 1825 Thomas Ashe noted in his Manx Sketch Book that *"the lead mines (are) now in active operation and contribute to the amusement of the curious visitor"*[3]. Thousands of people flocked to see the great Laxey Wheel in action but it was also popular to stop on the roads surrounding the Washing Floors and observe men, boys and a handful of women toiling away sorting lead ore[4].

Entertainment played a big part in Victorian Laxey. The annual highlight for all

Lively

"Laxey is becoming thickly populated, new houses, shops, hotels, public accommodations of all kinds are being built." (Mona's Herald, 16th Jan 1861)[1]

The Captain's Hill entrance to the Valley Gardens. From here tourists could watch the workers on the mine's washing floors.

Douglas to Laxey

Return trip Douglas to Laxey – car or carriage drawn by one horse, for four persons and the driver, 11s. Wagonette or other conveyance, for six persons and the driver, 16s. 6d. Sociable or long car, for ten persons and the driver, 22s. (Jenkinson's Practical Guide to the Isle of Man 1874) [2]

Laxey river was heavily polluted

Did you know?

In the old days Manx people used wool as a cure for warts. They would take a piece of woollen thread and tie as many knots upon it as there were warts. They then buried the wool or threw it away and as the wool rotted it was hoped the warts would also die away.

villagers was the late summer Fair held on the banks of the rivermouth where people from miles around could enjoy a day of feasting, trading and games. And there were plenty of year-round activities. Working men found a peaceful haven in the Reading Rooms set up in Old and New Laxey, while school and church halls played host to numerous choirs, societies, talks and festivals such as the Harvest Home or 'mhelliah' which culminated in the distribution of warm clothing, coals and groceries to poor families. Even parts of Captain Rowe's large grain warehouse on the harbour doubled as a gymnasium and concert hall. Music and dancing was enjoyed in many guises, from informal 'ceilidhs' (barn dances) to village bands.

Such distractions must have been welcome for the working class folk whose lives were undoubtedly hard. Large families were common, with eight to ten children the norm and many lived crammed into tiny cottages. Sadly, many children never made it to adulthood. Poor sanitation, polluted water supplies and hard working conditions meant children and adults were vulnerable to disease, infection and premature death. Medical care was provided by a district doctor but this had to be paid for and if a patient couldn't afford it they were sometimes helped out by wealthier parishioners. [5]

To help explain the unexplained many Laxey people placed great store on folklore. Various remedies were employed to prevent the 'little people' taking new born babies and elder trees were grown outside cottage doors to keep bad spirits away. Natural remedies and dye plants were common knowledge and tales of spirits, fairies and humans with special powers abounded.

Orthodox beliefs mainly took the form of Methodism which attracted many devout followers in Laxey, especially among the temperance movement. Miners and pubs were judged to be a volatile combination and efforts to curb the demon drink included the establishment of tee-total hotels such as Tupper's.

On a practical level, securing the basics of daily life involved constant effort. Laxey river was polluted by effluent and lead residue from the mines so fresh drinking water was largely drawn from the valley's numerous springs and wells, many of which were credited with magical healing powers – but this was presumably because well water was pure, unlike that in the river! Domestic lighting was provided by candles and gas lamps; sewage was collected in cesspools and ash pits which were emptied at night; and urine was often sold to farmers as fertiliser or fulling mills for treating woollen cloth.

Most provisions could be bought in the village but occasionally a long, roller-coaster journey to Ramsey or Douglas was required. This was remedied when seven miners, supported by hundreds of village shareholders, established the Laxey Industrial and Provident Co-operative Society in March 1870 [6]. The

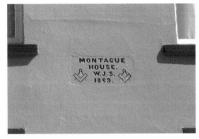

The original Laxey Industrial & Provident Co-operative Society premises, now the village chemist

Co-operative was a major supplier of groceries, and meat slaughtered locally at an abbatoir on the Glen Road. In fact the food available to villagers was generally more varied than the old image of 'spud 'n herring'. Laxey people wouldn't touch trout – perhaps because the river was so poisoned – but herring (known as 'Port St Mary steak') was just one of a range of seafoods caught in the bay, including mackerel, crabs, lobsters, scallops, winkles, red gurnard, cod, flat fish and oysters from a two mile long oyster bed just off Laxey Bay. Local farmers raised sheep and cattle, and most householders would bake their own barley bread, bonnag, soda cake, bun loaf and oatcakes and make their own butter and cheese from local milk. Liquid refreshment came in the form of buttermilk and 'jough', a home-brewed light beer drunk by the whole family.

Clothing in the early Victorian era was made to last as long as possible and good quality items were handed down, sometimes even bequeathed, from one generation to the next. These 'best' clothes usually only came out on Sundays or Fair Days. Everyday working clothes or 'wearing-clothes'[7] were generally worn until they fell apart, then cut

Traditional Manx countrywoman's dress

up and used for quilts and rag-rugs or sold to the rag-and-bone man. The main fabrics used were linen, wool and cotton and Laxey's paper makers were even known to recycle linen rags to make paper. Another popular fabric was 'linsey-woolsey', a warm, hard-wearing linen-wool mix in which the vertical threads were linen and the horizontal threads wool. This had many uses in clothing but was also used around the house, particularly for bedding, while heavier blankets were made up of undyed plain woollen cloth.

Woollens

'Blankets and all woollen stuffs were sold there and also flax waistcoats, which were fashionable wear for the men. Flax workers were numerous… Both wool and flax were sold in great quantities at the Fairs, especially at the 'City'. The Woollen Fair was famous, buyers coming from all parts to make purchases…'
('The Parish of Lonan' by Hilda Cowin)[8]

By the 1860s and '70s new draperies in Laxey, Douglas and Ramsey were trumpeting their imported and factory-made cloth, and Laxey's handful of cottage weavers mainly provided for farmers and miners whose needs were not so refined. In the 1860s woollen cloth could not be exported and much of it made its way to a major wool fair held every year at Agneash village, known as 'the City', high on the hills above Laxey Wheel.

Enter Egbert Rydings

In 1870 the future of Laxey's woollen industry was determined by the appearance of an imposing figure from Failsworth in Lancashire called Egbert Rydings. Egbert was 37 at the time, a big, humorous man with a strong Lancashire accent and, although he was a silk weaver by trade, his destiny was to lie with the St George's Woollen Mills.

Egbert's early life was typical of many urban children during the Industrial Revolution. Born in a crowded terrace near the

Egbert Rydings

busy Rochdale Canal, at the age of ten he had followed his father into working in a large silk factory. Over the next two decades he experienced all aspects of the trade, from weaving to design and bookkeeping, in the hope of becoming an overseer. During that time he married and had a son, Harold, but by the 1860s the silk industry was in decline and he sought to make quick money by investing in an iron foundry. Unfortunately, a disastrous fire – and no insurance – put paid to that plan and a decision was needed on what to do next.

The answer came with Egbert's wife Eleanor Callister, a Manx girl whose father farmed at Kirk Michael on the west coast of the Isle of Man. Egbert and Eleanor had been married on the Island and had their son christened there so it can't have taken much persuasion to move to a new life across the water. For the first year they had very little money and Egbert boosted their coffers by helping his father-in-law on the family farm. But then word began to reach them of the up-and-coming fortunes of a mining village on the Island's east coast. Before long the Rydings had upped sticks again and moved to Glen Road in Laxey.

The district they arrived in was ripe for new traders and it didn't take long for the couple to set up their own drapery business which Eleanor managed, while Egbert took on the posts of Manager and Secretary of the new Laxey Industrial and Provident Co-operative Society. Within a few years, aided by Egbert's shrewd property dealings and a substantial legacy of five hundred pounds, their financial situation had improved; a second son, Herbert, was born and life was on the up.

Sadly, in December 1874 Eleanor fell ill with a long, drawn out illness that left her weak and bedridden and the following year Egbert resigned his Co-op jobs and gave up the drapery in order to nurse her full time. On the advice of doctors, he moved the family to a sunnier location which was just two hundred yards from the Washing Floors. Here he could see female workers out in all weathers sorting lead ore – but his observations were hardly sympathetic:
"I have tried hard enough… to get a female to help take charge of (my wife) but I could not…and within 200 yards of our house are half a score of widow women – be-clogged and be-jacketed – from 7 o'clock in the morning to 6 at night, pushing, pulling and trundling heavy wheelbarrows… I know…that although most have brought up families, still they would be as useless about a sick person as a baby, and their heavy step and coarse touch would send distracted a poor feeble creature." [9]

14 New Road, Laxey, an early home of Egbert Rydings

During Eleanor's illness Egbert began reading the works of John Ruskin, the prominent Victorian writer and social reformer, and was greatly affected by Ruskin's philosophies on life and his attitudes towards industrialisation. In 1871 Ruskin had begun an open series of 'Letters to the Workmen and Labourers of Great Britain' or 'Fors Clavigera', and also founded the St George's Fund, later known as the Guild of St George, which promoted agricultural rather than industrial activity. In 1875 Egbert wrote to Ruskin with a query and, having had a personal reply, felt bold enough to write again a year later suggesting corrections to Guild accounts printed in Fors Clavigera. But it was the postscript to this letter that is of interest to our particular story. Knowing of Ruskin's interest in the value of handicrafts he mentioned that:

"There is a good deal of hand spinning done in this little Island but I am sorry to say that there are no young girls learning now to spin, and in a few years more the common spinning wheel here will be as great a curiosity as it is in Lancashire... home-spun 'Manks-made dresses' as they are called, last too long and therefore, do not give the young women a chance of having four or five new dresses in the year." [10]
Ruskin didn't take him up on the issue straightaway - but the seed had been sown.

John Ruskin in 1869

In referring to the Guild of St George accounts Egbert had shown himself to be adept with figures and Ruskin soon appointed him as the Guild's bookkeeper and treasurer. But this was only part-time work and Egbert still itched to stretch himself further, particularly in the field of textile manufacture for which he retained a real passion. In March 1876 he wrote to Ruskin asking to become a Guild Companion, which would allow him to share the benefit of his experience with others. Companions were basically the 'field workers' for the Guild of St George, putting Ruskin's philosophies about land, handicrafts and agriculture into practice...

"Although I have had 20 years of idleness from the work I served my apprenticeship at, still I feel that I could 'throw a shuttle' with a little practice as well as ever I could. I feel the craft of it still in my fingers and I believe it has not left me and if the Master ordered me to work at that 'calling' I would gladly do so." [11]

Egbert was duly appointed as a Companion but just one month later his beloved wife Eleanor died, aged forty-two. With no firm employment and two young sons to raise Egbert's life was at a crossroads once again.

Who Was John Ruskin?

The name John Ruskin may only be vaguely familiar to modern readers, but in Victorian Britain there would be very few people who hadn't heard of him. By the late nineteenth century he was known as one of Britain's greatest and most prolific writers, artists and social revolutionaries and the most influential art critic of the period. He had a remarkable influence on public opinion, especially in his views that money-making and manufacturing were taking over the landscape.

In 1864 Ruskin's father died, leaving young John a considerable fortune but his strong social conscience made him extremely generous with his wealth and throughout the rest of his life he subsidised many artistic, educational and social projects and gave away much of his money. His Guild of St George was an attempt to counter the ill effects of Britain's new industrial practices, enlisting the help of Companions to work its lands and 'Friends' to lend support. Guild funds consisted of Ruskin's own money and Companions' subscriptions which represented a portion of their income. The Guild was strictly hierarchical with Ruskin as the Master – but it was by no means male dominated. He had many close, often wealthy, female friends interested in doing 'good works' and the Guild was notable for its strong base of female supporters.

The aims of the Guild were quite clear - to value human skill over machinery and to educate working people in the natural sciences, history and the arts. The only permitted machinery in Guild enterprises was that powered by wind, water and later electricity. Steam was "absolutely refused, as a cruel and furious waste of fuel to do what every stream and breeze are ready to do so costlessly"[12]. It was this last stipulation which was to prove most critical to the plans of Egbert Rydings.

The Birth of a Woollen Mill

By 1861 the number of hand loom weavers in the Laxey area had shrunk to just half a dozen and woollen spinners were becoming equally scarce. Young men were seeking employment in the mining industry and young women were also being tempted by new job possibilities, especially those offered by the Island's exciting visiting industry.

In addition to this, consumers were demanding – and being supplied with – higher quality imported fabrics. Laxey drapers sold woollen cloth made in Lancashire and Yorkshire, while fine merino and cashmere could be found at the fancy draperies in Douglas. By the time of the 1871 Lonan census there were just a handful of 'spinsters' and two woollen weavers left in the entire district and as the decade progressed, Manx women in both town and country were being tempted by an 'itching desire for finery' [13]. As a trained hand loom worker Egbert Rydings observed the situation with concern. He realised that the women he'd seen working on the Washing Floors of the mines would, in times past, have been able to rely on spinning for income and he felt strongly that such handicrafts were too valuable to lose.

"..there is no trade in the whole range of handcrafts so clean, healthy and delightful as at-home hand loom weaving – and none in my humble opinion which come so near to the fine arts." [14] (Egbert Rydings to John Ruskin)

Manx clothes

'My eldest brother went to Liverpool to work dressed in Manx clothes. Mother had to get him an English suit as his cousins didn't like his coarse dress on Sundays.' [24]
(Memories of a Manx countrygirl in the 1840s)

Knowing that his concerns were shared by John Ruskin, and feeling adrift after the death of his wife, Egbert proposed to his Master a revival of cottage weaving and spinning. To his delight, Ruskin embraced the idea and in November 1876 Egbert received a cheque for £25 from the Guild of St George to support the spinning and cloth industry of the Isle of Man 'among its poorer inhabitants' [15]. Ruskin also told his readers that he hoped that a square yard of Laxey 'homespun' would be 'one of the standards of value in St George's currency" [16], inferring that Laxey cloth was to be the quality yardstick by which all goods should be measured.

The following winter Egbert eagerly rented a room in the village where young people could be taught spinning and weaving [17] but, unfortunately, quickly came up against the fundamental problem behind the demise of these crafts - that *'the material produced by the old spinning wheel was of such coarse texture that English ladies would not wear it. Its appearance was something like coarse sackcloth or ancient tapestry.'* [18]

Despite his best efforts Egbert soon realised that this material would never compete with the popular new imports and a revival of home spinning and weaving was something of a lost cause. Forced to think again he this time settled on a more workable compromise – to start up a small woollen mill based on Ruskin's principles. Here locals could find useful employment and learn new skills but a better quality of cloth could be produced using water-powered machinery.

As luck would have it, in the summer of 1879 Moughtin's Corn Mill came up for sale at the junction of the Glen Roy and Laxey rivers. The layout of the building and its lands made it ideal for Egbert's purpose and on the 6th August he purchased a quarter share, with the mill's neighbour Margaret Fargher, and a Liverpool joiner called William Kneale, buying the remainder. To make the mill suitable for woollen manufacturing required a substantial investment of five hundred pounds but Egbert was able to persuade the Guild to fund two thirds of the money needed and he provided the rest[19]. By November 1880, he had extended the mill on the north side to increase the floor space on all three levels and equipped it with a water-powered spinning mule, carding engine and condenser machine[20]. Various outhouses were set up and a large water wheel erected at the rear and enclosed in a limestone wheel house. Business was now ready to be carried out 'in accordance with the laws of trade laid down in the writings of John Ruskin Esq'.

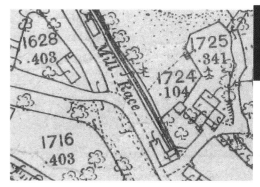

1869 Ordnance Survey Map. Moughtin's Mill is the L-shaped structure at the base of the Mill Race

Manx Clothing

Egbert certainly had a good market for his products in Laxey. Many of the male population at this time were involved in hard, outdoor labour – farming, fishing, construction and mining – and they would have all relied on wool for warmth and protection from the elements. Their woollen trousers, waistcoats, jackets and caps were often made from unfinished heavy wool flannel called 'kielter or kialter'. Finer, finished woollen suits in dark grey were known as 'yn cheeir lheeah'[21].

*Woollen Mills part-owner Margaret Fargher (2nd left) at Mona Ville. The mill is in the background.
Note the pet raven on the back of the chair!*

...*"Let this be thoroughly understood; we can never manufacture cloth that will compare in fineness and softness with machine made; ours will, as a consequence, be coarser and harder, and on that account more durable."* [22] (Egbert Rydings to John Ruskin)

Fishermen and farmers wore warm jerseys called ganseys and woollen gloves which kept the wearer warm even when wet, but the type of working clothes adopted by mine workers depended on the nature and location of their work. Men working underground wore canvas trousers and flannel shirts, while outdoor Washing Floor workers wore woollen trousers, waistcoats, jackets and flannel shirts.

*Laxey Snaefell Miners.
Their clothing had to be
very hard-wearing*

Manx nineteenth century clothing terms[23]
Giare-choot – a jacket or short coat
Cossag-varkiagh – a great coat or riding coat
Oanrey – a petticoat
Loaghtan – wool from the native Manx sheep
which varied from light brown to dark brown.
Keeir – dark, browny-black wool
Lheeah – grey cloth
Gorrym or gorriman – blue, a popular Manx
colour in the nineteenth century.
Keeir as lheeah –a blend of brown and grey
Keeir as gorrym – a blend of brown and blue
Oashyr-voynnee – a footless stocking with a
string under the foot.
Oashyr sloblagh – a stocking with no sole but
a lappet looped over the instep to the foretoe.

The colour of early Manx-made clothing was largely dictated by the natural dyes
available. Clothing made of the native Loaghtan wool was left undyed in its
natural tawny-brown but blue was so popular that it is often referred to as 'Manx
Blue'. Grey, green and black were also widely used and red was the favoured
colour for women's petticoats. Cloth wasn't always plain but often a blend of
colours in checked or striped combinations. Well-to-do Laxey residents had a
greater choice of fabrics but colours were still largely drab and dark, although
tweed was growing in popularity with the shooting and fishing fraternity who
favoured its warm earthy colours and practical style.

For a country woman working dress usually consisted of a full, dark coloured
skirt that fell a few inches above the ankle. Beneath this she wore one or more
petticoats, made of wool, linen or linsey-woolsey. Legs and feet were either bare
or covered with hand-knitted woollen stockings. The upper half of the body was
covered by a short woollen bodice and a loose linen jacket with a broad collar
called a 'bedgown'. For outdoor wear, a woollen shawl, known as a 'blanket',
was worn over the shoulders and tied at the back. In bad weather this could be
pulled over the head to keep the wearer warm and dry. Sunday-blankets were
kept for best wear – these were often made in a plaid or tartan design and for
many years it was a legal requirement that they be handed down to the next
female descendant[25].

As far as fashion goes this all sounds fairly unadventurous. But by the 1870s woollen cloth was no longer confined to staid, conventional clothing. Laxey beach was known for its clean, safe bathing waters and both men and women were taking to swimming in woollen serge or dark flannel bathing dresses, gradually replaced by two-piece belted costumes [26]. When dry these garments would have been considered incredibly daring and exciting – though they must have been pretty baggy and uncomfortable when wet!

Meanwhile, In Onchan

By 1880 the Laxey woollen industry was all set to move up a gear, but before this story can move on it's important to look at similar events taking place a few miles down the road in Onchan. There, hidden deep in undergrowth in a wooded glen, lie the remains of the Bowring Woollen Mill, a highly successful enterprise established by Yorkshireman James Forster in 1845. James was a woollen weaver from Armley near Leeds, one of the biggest woollen weaving centres in England. In the 1830s his eldest son George had moved to Douglas and set up as a woollen weaver at the top of Bigwell Street (now upper Lord Street). Shortly after, James also moved to the Island and purchased some land at Ballacain on the Kerroodhoo estate in Onchan. Here he built a small woollen mill which he worked with his other sons James and Francis and daughter Ann. Before long George joined the family at Ballacain and by the early 1860s they had expanded their workforce and built up a highly respected business supplying woollen cloth to drapers, tailors and local wool merchants through the mill and their own store in Athol Street.

In 1870 James snr. died, aged 89, and George took over the business, carrying on for another ten years and building a reputation that carried his name across the Island. By April 1880 he was ready to retire and sold off all his stock at the Bon Marche stores in Victoria Street, Douglas [27]. The land where the mill stood, however, was crucial to the linking of the new reservoirs being built to supply Douglas with fresh water and in June 1880 George accepted a generous offer from the Douglas Water Work Company for the land, mill buildings, plant and water rights. The land was sold and the mill was dismantled.

To Egbert Rydings, at that time setting up a new woollen mill in Laxey, this must have been a Godsend. Egbert is very likely to have known the Forster family

> **Did you know?**
> *Serge is a hardwearing woollen cloth used for overcoats and uniforms. Flannel was much softer and used for underwear and trousers.*
> *Worsted is a fine fabric used in men's suiting. It is usually made from long fleeced sheep and processed in a slightly different way to woollen yarn.*

through his drapery business and it's not hard to imagine that he benefited directly from the sale of the Bowring plant, machinery, water wheel and other fixtures and fittings. He also needed experienced woollen industry workers and for young James Forster, who lost both his home and job in the Onchan sale, the Laxey mill provided an unexpected opportunity. Within months James had moved his family to a new life in Laxey and the prospect of secure employment in the St George's Woollen Mill.

Egbert now had workers, a fully equipped mill and ready customers. It was time to open his doors.

References:
1. Mona's Herald, 16th Jan 1861, MNH
2. Jenkinson's Practical Guide to the Isle of Man, H. Jenkinson, Edward Stanford, London 1874
3. A Manx Sketch Book, Thomas Ashe, Douglas 1825
4. 'Our Own Guide to Laxey and its neighbourhood by a Resident' Dr John Bradbury, Tetlow, Stubbs & Co. Oldham 1876
5. 1890 report into Poor Relief, MNH
6. IOM Public Record Office, Company file 24/486
7. 'Manx Dialect' W. Walter Gill, Arrowsmith, 1934
8. 'The Parish of Lonan' Hilda Cowin, 1938 IOMNHAS V4 p.325
9. Egbert Rydings to John Ruskin, letter dated March 10th 1876, Ruskin Library
10. Egbert Rydings to John Ruskin, letter dated March 4th 1876, reprinted in the Manxman Nov 7th 1896 p.3 MNH
11. Egbert Rydings to John Ruskin, letter dated March 10th 1876, Ruskin Library
12. General Statement of the Nature & Purposes of St George's Guild 1882, John Ruskin, Ruskin Library
13. Egbert Rydings to John Ruskin, letter dated March 10th 1876, Ruskin Library
14. ibid
15. John Ruskin to Egbert Rydings, letter dated 7th November 1876, reprinted in the Manxman Nov 7th 1896. Also letter 72 (Dec 1876) Fors
16. Fors Clavigera V.VI, John Ruskin p.391 Ruskin Library
17. Egbert Rydings to John Ruskin, letter dated Dec 12th 1877 reprinted Mannin Vol.7 1916
18. The Manxman Nov 7th 1896, MNH
19. Egbert Rydings to John Ruskin, letter dated Oct 15th 1879, reprinted Mannin Vol.7 1916
20. St George's Woollen mill deeds
21. 'Historical and Statistical Account of the Isle of Man' Ch.XVII, Joseph Train, Quiggin Douglas 1845
22. Egbert Rydings to John Ruskin, letter dated June 1876
23. Ibid and Jeffcott, IOMNHAS Presidential address Yn Lioar Manninagh, Vol.1 p.153/8
24. 'Life in Ballaugh in the 1840s' Ellie Shimmin, Mannin No.5 p.269
25. 'The Isle of Man' Rev. J.G. Cumming, John Van Voorst, London 1848
26. Pauline Weston Thomas, www.fashion-era.com
27. IOM Times April 15th 1880, MNH

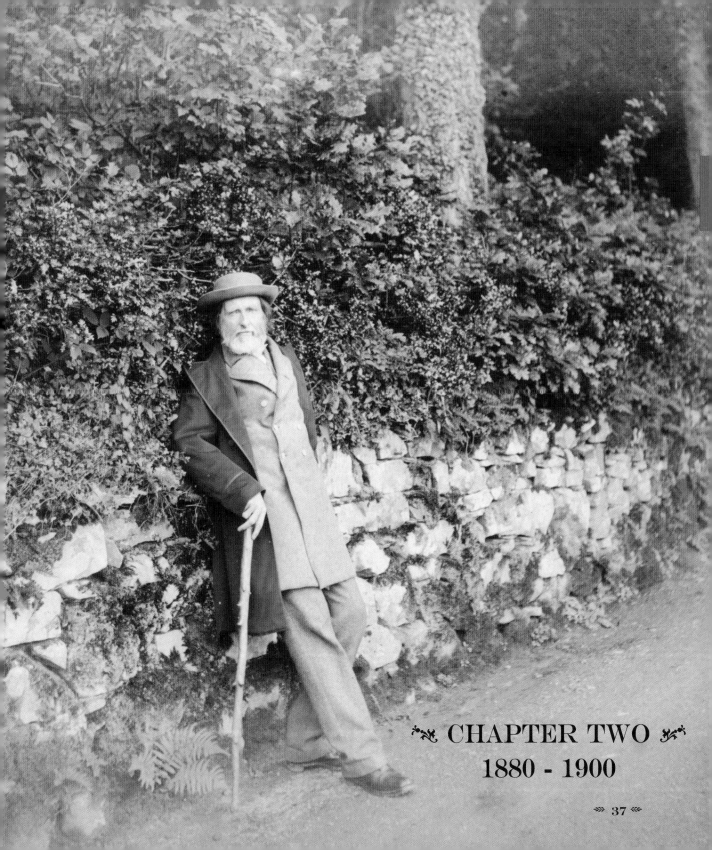

❧ CHAPTER TWO ❧
1880 - 1900

Timeline

1882   The Douglas, Laxey & Ramsey Railway company established

1882   The Mona Aerated Mineral Water company established in Laxey

1885   The Glenroy Cloven Stones Company established

1887   Jubilee Year. Over 300,000 visitors Island-wide

1887   onwards. A period of rapid recession for the mines

1888   The Gardens Hotel extension built at the entrance to the Glen Gardens

1890   Minorca Methodist Chapel built at a cost of £825

1891   Glen Road Methodist Church Hall constructed opposite the chapel

1894   Establishment of the Laxey Fishing Company

1894   Opening of the Douglas-Laxey electric railway

1895   February. Snow fell for 33 hours, blanketing the Island for many weeks

1895   Opening of the Snaefell Mountain Railway

1895   First election of Laxey Village Commissioners

1897   Snaefell Mine Disaster. Twenty miners killed by carbon monoxide gas

1898   Opening of the Laxey-Ramsey Electric Tramway

1898   Opening of the present Laxey MER station

Waiting for a tram at Laxey Station

Laxey for Industry — and Romantic Beauty

Laxey was a bustling centre of industry and progress in the 1880s. New skills and workers had been brought to the area by the mining of valuable metals and the construction of giant water wheels, tramways, bridges and roads. Down on the harbour small steamer ships plied a constant route bringing in grain, timber, coal and provisions, and taking away lead and zinc ore for export. Residents and visitors relied mainly on Crellin's fleet of horse drawn waggonettes for road transport but by the mid-1890s local newspapers were reporting that 'the motor car rage' had extended to the Island[1].

Laxey wasn't only known for industry, however. By 1880 it was already 'famous for its romantic beauty'[2] and ideally placed to capitalise on the hundreds of thousands of visitors who flocked to the Island over the next twenty years. Such numbers would have been a logistical nightmare if it hadn't been for the establishment of 'wakes weeks', a system in which whole towns of factory workers from England's north-west were required to take their week's holiday on specific dates. These dates were publicised in the annual Manx Year Books so Laxey landladies would have been able to plan for a certain number of visitors at any one time[3].

Tourism was becoming a highly organised business with many people jumping on the bandwagon. Garwick Glen, en route to Laxey, proudly advertised its 'Illuminated caves! Druidical stones! Ferns and Archways' and a company was even started up to promote the prehistoric cloven stones at nearby Glen Roy.

Holidaymakers wanting to take home a reminder of their time on the Island could now buy specially tailored souvenirs such as embroidered handkerchiefs, three-legged Staffordshire pottery teapots, Manx-made perfume called 'Mona's Bouquet' or a stick of locally made rock that, from 1888, had the Three Legs of Man running through the centre.

Laxey itself was keen to be seen as an alternative to Continental resorts, especially with the attractions offered by the celebrated Victoria Park which now boasted swings, quoits, hobby horses, croquet, an American Bowling saloon, bowling green and an impressive athletics track. By the end of the century the Park became the Laxey Glen Gardens, promoted as the 'Beauty Spot of Mona' and the

Laxey Glen Gardens

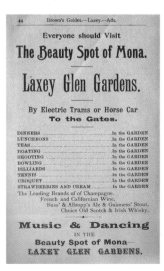

'Children's Paradise'. Hundreds of children at a time would often descend on the gardens for outings and annual picnics.

One area of the village that wasn't promoted to visitors was the Laxey river. In the 1880s it was polluted not only by lead from the mines but dye and washing residue from the new woollen mill and effluent from the Glen Road slaughterhouse. Clean water was still only available from springs and wells and, with the increasing population and huge visitor numbers, the new village Commissioners were urged to instigate a proper water supply[4].

Hobby Horses, Laxey Glen.

Having fun in Laxey Glen Gardens

Since the decline of the mines, Laxey "has gone in more fully as a restful holiday resort. There are several good hotels, and numerous comfortable restaurants and refreshment rooms for day visitors. Laxey Glen is traversed by the Laxey river - the Laxa, a contraction of 'salmon river' from the abundance of that much-prized fish in its waters before they were poisoned by the lead from the mines. The river is now at all times sadly discoloured by the outflow from the washing floors of the mines; and, by it, runs the glen road to the beach, bordered by trim, well-kept houses, most of them having pretty flower gardens in front, and large kitchen gardens in the rear. Opposite the St George's Mills, the streams from the two upper glens flow into each other; and the contrast between the bright, clear waters of the Glen Roy river and grey, muddy waters of the Laxey river as they escape from the mine workings, is very striking and suggestive." Brown's Directory 19th Edition[5]

In 1894 the village really opened up to visitors with the establishment of the Manx Electric Railway allowing travel between Douglas and Laxey in comfort and style. The following summer the tourist trail extended even further with the opening of the Snaefell Mountain Railway which carried nine hundred passengers every day in its first season![6] By the end of the century Laxey was becoming so busy that Egbert Rydings once referred to it as 'busy as Lourdes'[7].

To provide for the growing number of residents and visitors Laxey offered a large variety of shops, two banks and a market garden on Minorca Hill which produced a huge range of fruit and vegetables in four acres of land and three 100-foot long greenhouses. One of the few concessions to the housewife at this time was the regular delivery of food supplies. Fish, bread, Co-operative groceries, milk and post were delivered around the village by cart on a weekly basis which must have been a huge help.

Housing for ordinary workers remained fairly basic, and low income or single-parent families sometimes doubled up with other families. Many also took in lodgers, usually miners who lived and worked in Laxey during the week then walked home at the weekends. Insanitary housing conditions were blamed for high incidences of typhoid and scarlet fever and in 1891 local government were forced to improve more than eighty properties[8]. By contrast, wealthier Laxey residents were investing in grand detached Victorian houses with views of the hills and sea, domestic staff, gardeners – and the very latest in indoor washing and toilet facilities.

Working life for poorer families generally started at an early age and continued for as long as you were physically able. Labourers and lead miners often worked well into their sixties and seventies – if they lived that long – but the number of men employed in the Laxey mines fell away rapidly after 1887[9]. In the early 1880s many Laxey women were occupied outside the home, as housekeepers, cooks, dressmakers, dairymaids, stocking knitters, school mistresses, domestics and, as we shall see later, woollen mill workers[10].

Despite the long hours and tough nature of many Laxey occupations, villagers still found the time and energy for a range of activities. Walking was both a necessity and a leisure pastime. Cycling was the new 'big thing' for both men and women, and athletics, swimming and boxing were all popular, as well as a type of hockey called 'commag'. The local rugby team trained on rough farmland but were still good enough to compete in matches all over the Island. When rugby-playing miners left to find work in South Africa, football took over in popularity – mainly because the team didn't require so many men![11]

If you weren't interested in sport Laxey offered plenty of other recreational interests, from ploughing matches to brass bands. Or you could improve your intellect by joining the Laxey Mutual Improvement Society for recitals, poetry readings, singing, lectures and outings to places of historical interest. Women who had the luxury of leisure time enjoyed making home furnishings such as fire-screens, cushion covers and anti-macassars with an ornate tapestry known as 'Berlin wool'. Even in simple cottages it was noted that the Manx had 'an exceptional genius for decorative art as applied to the surroundings of the home'[12].

Church festivals were frequent and well attended and in late 1892 the Laxey Church Lads' Brigade started up for boys aged between 12 and 18. One of the attractions of church socials was probably the surprisingly grand food available which, on occasion, included pigeon, chicken, stubble goose, beef, mutton and veal and even puffin coated with spices and vinegar[13].

The Changing Face of Fashion

Women's dress experienced some dramatic changes in the late nineteenth century. Practicality was still important but exciting new styles, colours and fabrics were becoming more readily available and Manx newspapers regularly featured articles describing the colours and styles worn by elegant women of the time. Laxey's well-to-do could now spend glamorous evenings at the new theatres and ballrooms of Douglas attired in the latest smart woollen frock coats, three-piece dress suits, capes and dress shawls.

New modes of transport and sporting activities also required new types of clothing. Bracing outdoor journeys on Laxey's open air trams and horse-drawn carriages called for the warmth of woollen knee and travel rugs, and the craze for cycling in the Isle of Man saw an upsurge in lightweight woollen skirts, bloomers and knee-length breeches. In 1878, a German Professor Gustav Jaeger had published a book claiming that only clothing made of animal hair, such as wool, promoted health and this did wonders for the wool industry. Cricket players made

1883 Bill of Sale - Daniel Corrin, Linen and Woollen Draper. The Cloth Hall and General Drapery Emporium, Douglas Selling to Mr Qualtrough of Port St Mary, crepe, cashmere, merino, linen, alpaca, silk, braid, buttons, umbrellas, gloves and one cloth suit £4.4s.6d

Young men of Laxey, Mines Road c. 1890

a ready market for white woollen jumpers, athletes needed lightweight woollen singlets and swimmers braved the water in sleeveless one-piece woollen costumes.

Everyday wear for middle and upper class Manx women generally consisted of dark coloured long woollen skirts, silk or cotton blouses and fitted woollen jackets, with long, heavy woollen capes for outdoor ventures. Ordinary folk trying to get around were exposed to all weathers, so clothing, especially outdoor clothing, had to be waterproof, warm and sensible. Woollen skirts, linsey-woolsey petticoats and woollen blanket shawls were still the norm for countrywomen, while young girls wore either dresses or long skirts covered with a pinafore. All men wore woollen cloth in some form or another, especially waistcoats, cloth caps and trousers for working men, and three-piece suits, knee-length coats and capes for 'gentlemen'. Young men and boys wore knee length woollen breeches with long woollen stockings, flannel shirts and single-breasted jackets. Dark colours were the norm with grey being especially popular.

On a more sombre note, the Victorian era was remarkable for a marked escalation in mourning dress. Following the death of Queen Victoria's beloved husband Prince Albert, she spent the rest of her days wearing black and this spawned a huge supporting industry. Black became the colour for funerals and defined the status of widows throughout the country. Sadly, the appearance of mourning dress in Laxey was all too common at this time due to high mortality rates resulting from disease, pollution, industrial accidents and sheer hard work.

"(Farmers) bring their wool to me and, either I manufacture it into cloth flannel or blankets – or any other material they want, or they give the wool to me and I give them manufactured goods in exchange for it." [14]
Egbert Rydings

The Mill Venture

The years 1880 to '81 were busy years for aspiring woollen manufacturer Egbert Rydings. With money lent by the Guild of St George he continued his building programme by constructing a single storey dye house attached to the north side of the mill and, next to that, a narrow two-storey 'drying shed' with long slatted wooden windows. By the middle of 1881 the modest little mill building was transformed and operating as a fully functional manufactory.

To honour the Guild's faith in him Egbert was determined to abide by four clear 'rules' set down by John Ruskin. That all material used in the manufacture should be of the best and purest quality; that finished goods must be 'as perfect as fingers can make them'; that anyone should be able to buy pure wool products direct from the mill, and finally, no credit – 'it will save sleepless nights' [15].

This section of the mill was originally the 'drying shed' The right hand section was the site of the dye house

The insistence on using pure wool to produce 'honest cloth' was a vital part of Ruskin's creed. Nineteenth century woollen manufacturers often added other sub-standard materials such as recycled cotton or linen rags into their yarn and sold the resulting cloth in three grades – mungo, jerry and shoddy. Sometimes entire

The rear of the St George's Woollen Mills (middle of picture) c.1900. The wheelhouse can be clearly seen to the left of the chimney

factories were given over to the manufacture of 'shoddy' but it was never as strong as cloth made from pure wool and quickly gained a bad reputation, hence the use of the word in modern times to describe poor quality goods.

In July 1881 Egbert made a trip to Brantwood, John Ruskin's home at Coniston Water in the Lake District, to update the Master on his progress and took with him a rough sketch of the newly extended mill. On seeing nothing more than a plain, rectangular, unpretentious factory Ruskin playfully scribbled beneath the picture 'First achievement of the St George's Company in Romantic architecture'. Nevertheless, he was still proud enough to frame the sketch and hang it in his drawing room at Brantwood where it stayed for many years [16].

Brantwood, John Ruskin's Lake District home

Egbert Rydings' sketch of the extended St George's Woollen Mill

Making the Cloth

The manufacturing process in the new St George's Woollen mill was a long, complex procedure consisting of many different stages. It began with local farmers delivering their raw fleeces into a long, low wool store where it was sorted, usually by women, who removed any clumps of dirt, grass and burrs and graded it according to colour and quality. It was then set aside ready for washing in the scouring shed in large vats of hot water, set over fires of dry gorse. Farmers sometimes used arsenic in their sheep wash and this had to be removed, along with the sheep's natural grease and any clinging dung and mud. To ensure thorough cleaning the wet wool had to be agitated with soap made from soapwort or from natural fats and oils boiled with caustic soda. The fleece was then squeezed in clean water and dried, and wool to be coloured was taken into the mill's new dye house (see section on dyeing).

A typical early Manx woollen mill's wool store

Unfortunately both the scouring and dyeing contributed to the appalling state of the lower Laxey river as the chemical-laden waste water was emptied directly into the river via a drain hole in the floor. Even Egbert himself later alluded to the state of the river as "a liquid slime"! [17]

The outfall from the mill's early dye house came out at the base of the river wall

The next processes took place in the main factory building and these required power supplied by a water wheel. The water supply for the wheel was diverted off the Laxey river just below the Washing Floors via a narrow, manmade lade or mill race. This ran diagonally underground and emerged in the mill yard where it was channelled into a wooden trough called a launder and carried to the wheel. For the wheel to maintain constant speed the water supply had to be regulated so it was collected in a small dam controlled by a sluice-gate. Once the water had done its job it flowed back into the river via a drain beneath the Glen Road.

The water wheel that Egbert used was put up in 1880. No records of it survive but a typical wheel of that era would have had a cast-iron frame, spokes, oak buckets and a leather belt from the drive wheel to the metal overhead line shafts. The remains of the shafts can still be seen on the

The channel for the race carrying water to the wheel

Rear of St George's Woollen Mills showing the remains of the line shaft mechanisms

Spinning Wheel

'Today (the spinning wheel) is as much a relic of a decayed instrument of trade in the Isle of Man as in Lancashire. There is still an old spinning wheel in the mill but it is not used; the mule does the whole of the spinning' [18].
The Manxman Nov 7th 1896

exterior wall. The power generated by the wheel was conducted through the mill by a complex series of steel line shafts and flat leather pulleys. When the mill was in full production the noise of these belts flapping at high speed must have added considerably to the deafening atmosphere.

To prepare the wool for spinning it had to be carded and this was a much more industrialised process than domestic carding. The wool was placed on the large rollers of a giant carding engine that moved it over hundreds of short metal spikes. Young boys were often put in charge of these machines and gruesome accidents were not unknown.

To help the wool pass smoothly over the cards it was often oiled, but this too proved hazardous, as the oil produced a mist of fine oil droplets known as Card Room Fog which could cause severe skin irritation.

Although Egbert may have initially trialled the spinning of some yarn with a spinning wheel, the quality and quantity produced was simply not satisfactory and most of it was spun on a mechanised spinning mule, which could produce vast quantities of high quality yarn in a fraction of the time. The word 'homespun' was still used to describe the cloth manufactured at the mill but it appears to have been little more than a promotional catchphrase implying plain, hard-wearing goods.

The weaving of the spun yarn also placed Egbert in something of a quandary. Experienced hand loom weavers in Laxey were thin on the ground and few men were willing to learn the trade. He also knew that a single water-powered loom could match the output of between four and six hand looms. In order to produce the amount of cloth needed to make the business a going concern Egbert therefore borrowed £200 from a Scottish acquaintance for additions to the mill including 'two power looms', a move that was unfortunately at odds with Ruskin's philosophies of 'arm over machine'. Even Rydings great friend, the Manx poet Thomas Brown passed comment on the unusual development *"Ruskin was primarily interested in our mountain handloom weavers. But he started this mill, a powerloom concern. Obviously it has no tendency to encourage, but rather to kill off the poor old things with their primitive domestic industry"* [19].

Once the woven cloth was taken off the loom it was sent to a local fulling mill to be 'finished' and returned to the mill for drying. To prevent dyed, patterned cloth from fading it was dried indoors on wooden racks or heated pipes in the two-storey 'drying shed'. This was actually a solid, stone building with long, vertical windows covered with angled wooden slats that kept out the sun but allowed air to circulate. Un-dyed cloth and white blankets would be dried outdoors on wooden tenter frames in the mill yard and in the Miller's field across the river. Tentering must have been back-breaking work. Much of the water would be squeezed out in a large mangle but the damp cloth was still heavy. This was wheelbarrowed alongside the tenter frames then handed up to other

'Tentering' damp woollen cloth at Sulby Woollen Mill. The same process was used in Laxey

workers, often women, who leaned over and stretched it onto the hooks and secured it to the bottom edges. If it rained (as is not unusual in the Isle of Man!) the cloth would all have to be brought in again.

When the cloth was completely dry it would be taken up to the mending room. There, young girls with good eyesight and nimble fingers, checked it for minor faults and tied off loose ends with a special knot to prevent the fabric unravelling. Mending was a highly skilled task and good menders were vital to the finished quality of the cloth. Finally the cloth would be smoothed, the nap raised and the cloth carefully folded ready for sale.

A mending table

The Difference a Dye Makes

By the late Victorian era dyeing was an integral part of the woollen business. Grey was a very popular colour which could be achieved by blending natural black wool with white, but the desire for clothing in colours other than grey or brown made dyeing a sought-after process. In 1880 imported dyes were replacing more subtle homegrown dyes and the discovery of new synthetic dyes soon increased the range of colours available.

"Mr Rydings…has secured against all chance of failure in colour or quality by acquainting himself with the honest and safe processes of dyeing. He is certain now of being able to deliver stuffs which can be depended upon absolutely for the lasting both of material and colour" [20]. John Ruskin 1881

The Laxey mill's dye house was a single storey facility located between the main manufactory and the drying shed. A typical dye house of the period would be furnished with a number of large metal vats standing on a flagged floor supported by bricks on either side, with a fire underneath and a bottom tap for emptying [21]. After dyeing the used dye water was flushed out of the dye house straight into the river via a drain hole (which can still be seen). The room was vented by a single tall chimney.

An industrial mangle for squeezing large pieces of wet cloth

Dyeing was an art in itself, requiring years of experience to achieve consistent tonal balance and true colours that wouldn't wash out or fade. But it was also hot, steamy and dangerous and left you with permanently stained skin and an unpleasant lingering smell from processing fermented plant dyes such as woad and indigo. Indigo had to be treated with sulphuric acid, making it particularly precarious to work with.

Indigo and woad both produced blue but they eventually fell out of favour following the discovery of 'mauve aniline', the first commercially produced synthetic dyestuff. However, although synthetic dyes brought progress for the manufacturer they also led to an increase in bladder cancer amongst dyers.

Other colours useful to the dyer included yellow which could be created from many locally grown Manx plants, in particular weld, known by the Manx as wullee-wuss. Green is a difficult colour to obtain from natural dyes but it could be created from a combination of weld and woad or indigo.

Red was commonly used in early Manx clothing especially for women's petticoats and often woven in combination with blue and green for tartan patterns. A number of plants gave varying shades of red but the most effective was obtained from the roots of the madder plant – an age old dye used by the ancient Greeks and Romans. Unfortunately, madder could cause nasty skin rashes – in the wearer as well as the person doing the dyeing!

Black was obtained either by using the wool of black sheep or by using an imported dye called logwood. This came specifically from a tree grown in America which was processed into a fine powder. Logwood was very versatile, allowing shades ranging from pale grey to intense blue-black, making it a useful dye in the Victorian era when grey was popular for suiting and black was fashionable for mourning dress.

Health and Safety

yeing was not the only risky undertaking in a nineteenth century woollen mill. No matter how sympathetic Egbert was to his workers their daily routine was subject to a 'health and safety' nightmare.

The first hazard was constant noise from flapping pulleys and belts, rotating machines and even the swoosh of the water wheel. The moving belts, looms and machinery also brought the constant danger of catching hands, hair or clothing. Then there was the potential for burns and slippery floors from the chemicals used in various parts of the building such as soda ash, caustic soda, sulphuric acid, mechanical oils and lubricants.

Weaving rooms were usually hot, noisy and humid and the air was filled with fine fibre particles. The clattering of the looms, especially power looms, could quite literally be deafening and chronic hoarseness was a side effect of constant shouting. Weaving operatives had to sit or stand in deep concentration for long hours and this must have given rise to aching arms and feet.

Respiratory diseases such as pneumonia, tuberculosis, bronchitis, phthisis and asthma from the lint and fibre dust were common and the inflammatory nature of wool dust was known to trigger allergic skin diseases. A particularly unpleasant type of tuberculosis known as scrofula, or 'King's Evil', was also associated with textile mills. This affected the lymph nodes in the neck, producing a highly disfiguring mass of pale blue swellings. Cases amongst children are noted in the Lonan census.

Male spinning operatives were also prone to cancer of the scrotum, which became known as 'mule spinner's disease' as it derived from the mule spinner's private parts coming into close contact with the mineral oils used on the mule[22].

The Mill Workers

During this early period in the mill's working life, Egbert was paid a small Manager's salary by the Guild of St George and he employed about twenty mill hands to work for him, ranging from teenagers to the over-sixties. This was something of an achievement as there was a 'great demand for labour in connection with the successful visiting industry and the consequent difficulty in obtaining it for other industries'[23]. But it seems he was willing to take on many villagers who were otherwise considered 'unemployable'. He later confided to a fellow Guild Companion that *"it has always been considered here that St George's Mill has been a sort of hospice, for the poor widdows (sic), orphans, deaf and dumb and cripples in the parish and have no doubt I have been the means of saving the Poor Rates of our parish"*[24].

The first person to be officially recognised as an employee of the St George's Woollen manufactory was a 45 year old widow called Elizabeth Clucas[25] who is listed in the 1881 Lonan census as a wool sorter. Another sorter was single mother Isabella Callow who lived with her daughter in a two room cottage, two hundred yards away on Mylrea's Terrace (since demolished) at the bottom of Captain's Hill.

The most important employees in Egbert's early years were probably James Forster and his family who had come from the Bowring Mill in Onchan. Between them they brought a lifetime of experience in the woollen trade which to Egbert, whose background was in silk, must have been invaluable. James started out as a spinner and weaver but ended up as Egbert's mill manager. His wife Elizabeth and 12 year old son Tom also worked as spinners and weavers, and in 1889 his

A panoramic view of Glen Road, Laxey, c.1890. The feature on the far left opposite the woollen mills is possibly horizontal tenter frames

older son John James was drafted into the mill, firstly as a woollen spinner and carder and later as a dyer and weaver.

Another of Egbert's longest serving employees was Margaret Kewley, a Manx-speaking widow who was possibly one of his first 'rescue' women. Margaret started out as a wool spinner and ended up working as a dyer in the mill for over twenty years.

One of the most notable things about Egbert's workers is that many were bi-lingual. English was well established as the Island's main language, but a number of older people still spoke Manx and there was also a curious blend of Manx Gaelic and English called Anglo-Manx dialect. This was basically English liberally coloured with Manx words and phrases and delivered in a distinctive Manx 'accent'. Some elements still linger today, such as the use of 'laik' at the end of a sentence.

Egbert was described as 'filled with sympathy and enthusiasm for the honest working folk with whom he spent his life'[26] and some of them stayed with him for more than two decades. He apparently paid good wages and the mill was advanced for its time, being lit throughout with electric light generated by a water-powered dynamo. Towards the end of the century a local newspaper described how the mill's workpeople 'follow their vocation under the best possible circumstances'. However, it then went on to say how they started work at 'seven o'clock each morning, finishing for the day at half-past six'[27] – an eleven and a half hour day, which must have been exhausting!

A Man of Many Talents

In the 1880s, with the mill up and running, Egbert Rydings found new personal happiness with marriage to a young English woman called Catherine Traylen, twenty-four years his junior. In 1887, when he was in his fifties, they had a daughter, Kathleen, and with both her older brothers having left home she was able to claim all her father's attention. Egbert was extremely musical and right from an early age it was apparent that Kathleen had inherited his musical abilities, showing exceptional talent for the violin. She later became an Associate of the Royal College of Music and went on to become one of the Isle of Man's foremost violin teachers and orchestra leaders.

The great Manx poet Thomas Edward Brown, a close friend of Egbert Rydings

In 1890 Egbert had a large, imposing detached house built for his new family. 'The Firs', possibly named after 'Firs Mill' in Failsworth, stands high on Rencell Hill on the southern slopes of Laxey and from its landscaped gardens Egbert could not only see the sea but look down on his beloved Mill buildings, just a ten minute walk away down a steep track.

Here he could also indulge in many of his other passions. Along with a head for business and fondness for music Egbert was a gifted writer, keen debater and fine singer, and during the period 1880 to 1900 he became friendly with many of the writers, artists and musicians at the heart of the Island's cultural revival. On a local level he pursued his passion for culture through the Laxey Mutual Improvement Society[28] by giving singing recitals and lectures on subjects ranging from evolution to socialism. But he was also encouraged to write by his two great friends, the Manx poet Thomas Edward Brown and the writer Hall Caine.

Egbert first met Brown during the summer of 1889 when Brown called at the St George's mill to order a dresspiece for one of his daughters. The pair soon began

corresponding and a deep friendship developed between the two men. Both were keen champions of the Anglo-Manx dialect and Egbert would send stories he'd written to Brown for his approval, although Brown once said *"I feel that Mr Rydings is easily my master in this dialect and that I can learn much from him"*[29]. In 1895 Egbert penned a collection of 'Manx Tales' written partly in dialect which reflect his love of his adopted homeland and feature plenty of references to Laxey and woollen cloth.

Hall Caine, a keen supporter of the Laxey Woollen Mills

Hall Caine was a fellow devotee of John Ruskin and his ten year correspondence with Egbert indicates a true marriage of minds. Later Caine referred to the big Lancastrian as "a very dear, loyal and true friend."

Egbert was also widely appreciated for his business acumen. In 1896 the Manx Government appointed him to a Commission of Enquiry on Local Industries, set up to discover why the fishing industry was in decline. They also sent him to Ireland to assess the viability of methods used by their butter factories and creameries.

All of which would make you wonder how he found the time to run a busy woollen mill. But this was Egbert's 'raison d'etre' and he made strenuous efforts to ensure its success.

Putting Laxey on the Map

When Egbert opened the doors to his new manufactory he faced quite a bit of competition for his products from local draperies and the Co-operative, which sold woollen socks, blankets and counterpanes supplied by a large Lancashire mill. But the lifting of long-standing restrictions on Manx wool exports meant he was soon able to set up a mail order business and in the second year of operation he produced a three page sales flyer advertising the Mill's 'good stock of cloth, tweeds, homespun serges, flannels, blankets, yarns, stockings etc.'. The flyer featured an endorsement from the Manchester Ruskin Society which praised his reliance on water power and encouraged support for the venture [30].

However, Manx people were quick to complain that Laxey cloth was too hard wearing, doing them out of the chance to indulge in new dresses and suits, and fellow Companions across the water didn't seem keen to buy cloth that was basically unexciting. Egbert reacted by warning Ruskin he would refuse to take any more salary unless he had greater support from the Guild and this seemed to do the trick. Shortly afterwards an article on the mill was published in the influential newspaper the Pall Mall Gazette [31] and the mill was swamped with orders.

Six years on business was going so well that Egbert was ready to take some major steps forward. On the 30th May 1891, with shareholder support from a number of successful Manx drapers and merchants, he established the St George's Mill Company Ltd., and twelve months later decided to extend the Mill's profile by taking a display stand at the Island's exciting International

Catalogue of the 1892 International Exhibition in Douglas

Exhibition on the outskirts of Douglas. Here, in a vast exhibition hall equipped with ventilating systems and electric and gas lighting, the Mill set up amongst two hundred exhibitors from all over the British Isles showcasing a wide range of goods such as mineral water, electric embroidery machines, Irish stout, preserved fruits, Manx limestone and even Russian furs.

Before long three-quarters of the mill's products were finding ready customers in England, America and the Continent. But this may not have been all that it seemed. A Manx newspaper noted rather cynically that most locals "discarded" Laxey's homespun cloth and it was favoured only by local celebrities connected with John Ruskin and his hundreds of worldwide readers [32].

Still, such connections didn't do the business any harm. In 1899 the Reverend John Quine (admittedly a close friend of Egbert's!) wrote that St George's homespun was being supplied 'to the élite of the artistic and aesthetic world of London...' [33]

Displayed

"A lady friend tells me that she was up in London the other day and saw displayed in one of the leading clothier's shop windows suit pieces and dress stuffs manufactured at St George's Mill, Laxey. Enquiry revealed the fact that the material was now being bought and worn by some of the leading ladies and gentlemen in the Metropolis". (The Manxman Dec 19th 1896)

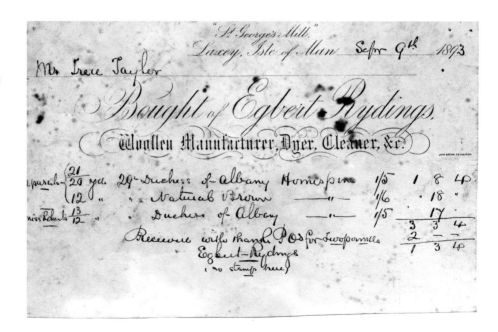

The Influence of Ruskin

John Ruskin didn't just pay lip service to the St George's Woollen Mill – from the 1880s to the turn of the century he and his secretaries set the example and wore suits made of Laxey material[34]. And they obviously lasted well. When the mill was first established, Egbert presented Ruskin with a suit of clothes made from Laxey 'homespun' and about seven years later an elderly lady came to the mill asking for some of the same cloth 'that Mr Ruskin wears going around Coniston'. Egbert replied that Ruskin did once get his cloth there but he had only had one suit and that was many years ago. "Yes" she replied "that's the one he still wears"![35]

Reputation

'Wherever John Ruskin's works have circulated – and who can define their area – there has been spread the name and reputation of the Laxey Woollen Mill'
(The Manxman Nov 7th 1896)

Sadly for Ruskin, his frail health made it increasingly impossible for him to take an active interest in the mill's affairs and in 1884 he entrusted direction of the Laxey venture to Guild Companion George Thomson, a forward-thinking woollen manufacturer from Huddersfield[36]. While it's probable that Thomson helped Egbert with practical advice there is no evidence that he ever visited Laxey or played anything other than a distant administrative role on Ruskin's behalf. Likewise, there is no record of Ruskin himself ever visiting the Isle of Man to see the St George's mill 'in the flesh'. He was already suffering ill health by the time the mill was established – and was known to be a very bad sailor so was probably daunted by the Irish Sea crossing.

John Ruskin died at Brantwood on the 20th January 1900 and later that year Egbert received a letter from a fellow Guild companion Mrs Fanny Talbot who opined that the Laxey Mill concern was a 'total failure'. Somewhat surprisingly he replied that on a business level it probably was. *"I have worked the Mill on the lines laid down by Mr Ruskin when the mill started 20 years ago and I find myself at least £200 poorer than I was when I commenced the business"*. But, he was keen to point out, *"it has been a great blessing for the poor people who have been working in the mill – most of them having been with me for 15 to 20 years and been getting good wages all the time…This of course is the great consolation to me that if I am poorer materially I hope I am richer spiritually"* [37].

John Ruskin at Brantwood

Egbert continued to work the mill until 1901 when age finally caught up with him. A new era was about to begin.

References:
1. The Manxman Nov 7th 1896, MNH
2. Brown's Directory, Brown & Sons, IOM Times Office, Douglas 1881
3. 'A Present From…' by Larch Garrard, David and Charles, 1976
4. The Manxman Aug 29th 1896, MNH
5. Brown's Directory 19th Edition Publ. Brown & Sons, IOM Times Office, Douglas p.226
6. The Manx Electric Railway Official Guide Centenary Year 1993
7. Letter Egbert Rydings to Rev. John Quine, August 7th 1897, Mannin
8. Local Government Board report 1891, MNH
9. 'The Isle of Man - A Study In Economic Geography' by J.W. Birch, Cambridge University Press 1964
10. 1881 Lonan census
11. 'Village Memories of David Boreland – Prominent Laxey Resident from 1879-approx 1965' Ramsey Courier 22nd June 1962 p.6, MNH
12. 'Exhibition of old Manx textiles' K. Williamson, IOM Ex March 22 1940, MNH
13. Manx Church magazine October 1891, MNH
14. Egbert Rydings to John Ruskin, letter dated Dec 9th 1882 Mannin Vol.7 p.407
15. The Home of "Ruskin Homespun" Laxey', extract from 'Mercantile Manxland 1900' Representative Business Houses of the Period in the Isle of Man publ. by The Mercantile Reviewing Co. London p.29, MNH
16. The Works of John Ruskin, Ed. Cook & Wedderburn, 1907 V.XXX Appendix Pl.xxxix facing p.331. Ruskin Library, Lancaster University
17. 'Manx Tales' Egbert Rydings, John Heywood, Manchester 1895 p.21
18. 'The Manxman' Nov 7th 1896 p.3, MNH
19. Letters of T.E. Brown V.II, Archibald Constable & Co, London, 1900
20. John Ruskin 1881 Master's Report 6th Dec, Ruskin Library, Lancaster University
21. 'Industrial Archaeology' A. Raistrick Eyre Methuen, London 1972 p.107
22. 'Journal of Industrial Medicine' Lee & McCann 1967 April V.24 pp148-151
23. Report of the Commission of Enquiry on Local Industries 1900, IOM Government MNH Library B.240
24. Letter Egbert Rydings to Fanny Talbot, letter dated 10th December 1900, Ruskin Library, Lancaster University
25. 1881 Lonan census
26. IOM Weekly Times April 20th 1912, MNH
27. The Manxman Nov 28th 1896, MNH
28. Mona's Herald March 20th 1895, MNH
29. Preface to 'Manx Tales', Egbert Rydings, John Heywood, Manchester 1895
30. Third Annual Report of the Manchester Ruskin Society, dated Feb 13th 1882. Reprinted in The Works of John Ruskin, V.30 Ed E. Cook and A. Wedderburn, George Allen, London 1907 Appendix p.332
31. 'St George's Cloth' Pall Mall Gazette, Feb 8th 1886, reprinted in 'The Works of John Ruskin' V.XXX ed. E.T. Cook and A. Wedderburn, George Allen 1907 pp.330-332, Ruskin Library
32. Manxman Nov 28th 1896 p.8, MNH
33. 'Handbook En Route – Isle of Man Souvenir of Coast and Mountain Electric Railways' Rev John Quine, IOMT&EP Co., 1899
34. "The Life of John Ruskin" W.G. Collingwood, Methuen, 1893
35. The Manxman Nov 7th 1896, MNH
36. 'Ruskin and Modern Business' W. Clarke, reprinted The Spectator 13th Feb 1900
37. Egbert Rydings to Fanny Talbot, letter dated Dec. 10th 1900 Ruskin Library, Lancaster University

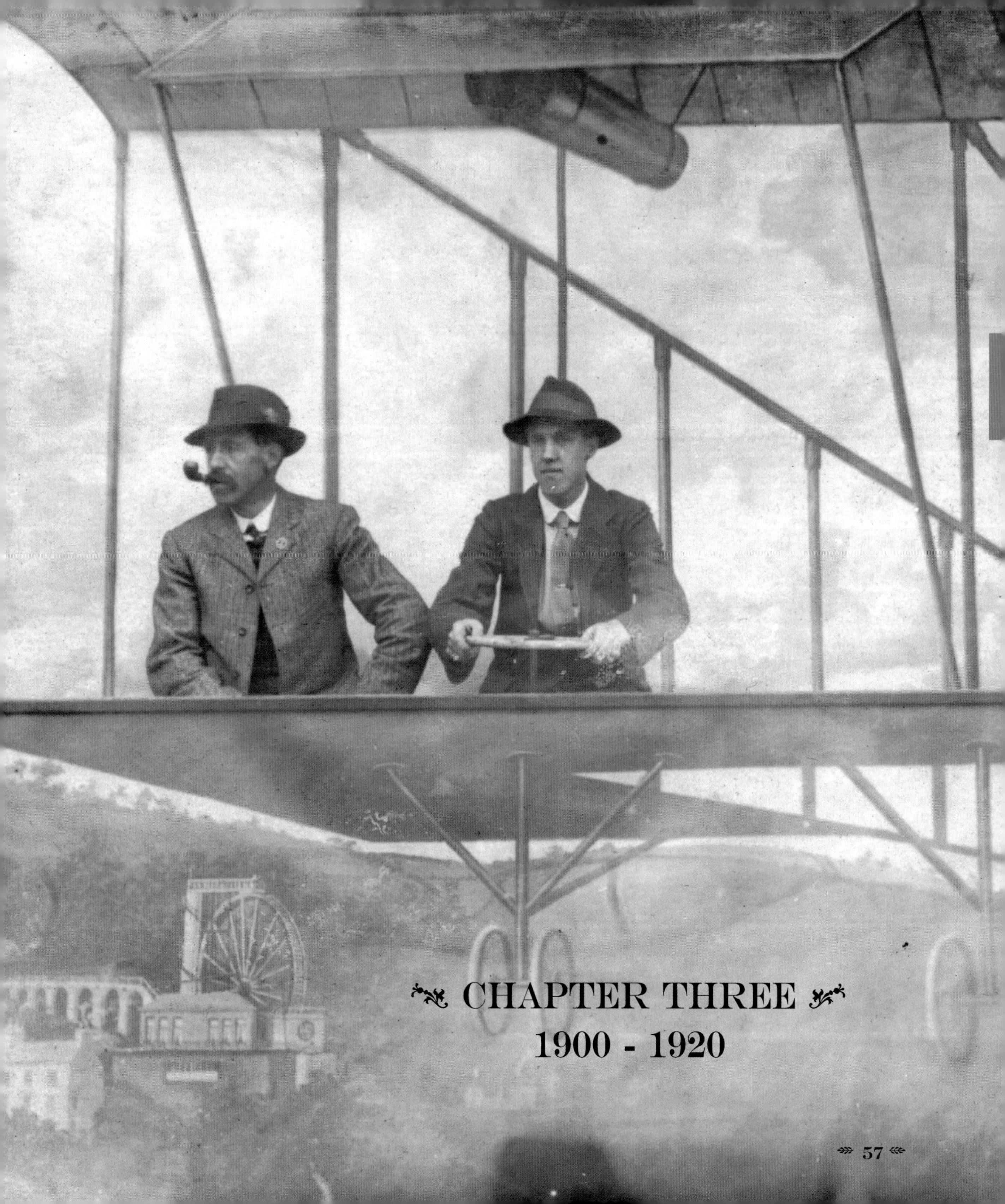

CHAPTER THREE
1900 - 1920

Timeline

1901	Death of Queen Victoria and accession of Edward VII, Prince of Wales
1902	August. Visit to the Isle of Man by King Edward VII and Queen Alexandra
1905	Fire virtually destroyed the Queen's Hotel on New Road
1905	Laxey granted a district nurse, paid for by the Noble's Trust
1905	Serious accident on Mountain railway involving three tram cars
1906	Manx Electric Railway company took over the Laxey Glen Gardens
1906	Snaefell summit café built to replace an earlier hotel destroyed by fire
1906	Glen Road recreation ground donated to the people of Laxey by the trustees of Henry Bloom Noble
1907	Two day strike over wages by workers of the Great Laxey Mine
1907	Inaugural Tourist Trophy motorcycle races
1907	Manx Electric Railway began charabanc service to Snaefell
1908	Snaefell mine closed
1910	Death of Edward VII. King George V and Queen Mary take the throne
1913	Laxey Pavillion burnt down
1914-18	World War One
1917	Wooden refreshment room at Laxey MER station destroyed by fire
1917	In the face of anti-German sentiment, the British royal family changed their name from Saxe-Coburg-Gotha to Windsor
1919	Two Avro aeroplanes offered pleasure flights round Douglas Bay

Laxey beach in 1905

A New Century

The start of the new century was defined by the death of Britain's beloved Queen Victoria on the 29th of January 1901. Her passing was mourned across the Commonwealth and the customs and fashions surrounding grief and mourning now became even more keenly adopted. The Queen was succeeded by her larger-than-life son King Edward VII and just one year into his reign he and his wife Queen Alexandra paid a visit to the Isle of Man where they received a warm and enthusiastic welcome. But Manx people were probably glad of a distraction. In 1900 the failure of Dumbell's Bank had left hundreds of shareholders and depositors in financial ruin. Five bank workers sent to trial on fraud charges were found guilty and variously sentenced to penal servitude and imprisonment with hard labour.

Technological progress was continuing at a remarkable pace, most notably in the development of aeroplanes, balloons and motorised transport. Most significantly for the Isle of Man during this period was the advent of the Tourist Trophy motorcar and motorcycle races. Motorcar racing came first but it was the motorcycle that was to put the Island on the world stage. In 1907 the races were carried out on the Clypse circuit but four years later they incorporated the challenging Snaefell Mountain roads.

Private motor vehicles were still rare beasts but groups of travellers had a few types of hired transportation available to them, the most exciting being the new charabancs introduced to the Island in 1907 by the Manx Electric Railway Company. They were large, open-top vehicles seating a couple of dozen passengers – lovely on a sunny day, but uncomfortable and not much fun in bad weather! Knee rugs, which had been the friend of the horse-drawn coach traveller, now became a vital travelling companion to keep this new breed of motorist warm.

Manx Electric Railway charabanc, c. 1910. Warm clothes needed!

Culturally the Island was undergoing a resurgence of interest in Manx customs and folklore. Archibald Knox and John Miller Nicholson led a vibrant art scene and a number of Manx writers and poets began to enjoy wider audiences. English was now the dominant language in the Isle of Man, although the 1901 census shows about 4,400 people were still bi-lingual in Manx and English.

Snaefell Mountain Railway tram

From 1900 to 1914 the Island was still highly popular with English visitors who flocked to Manx shores in their hundreds of thousands – averaging half a million each year. By 1911 a disgruntled visitor was even prompted to describe a new dilemma for the Island - it was simply getting too busy! *'The Isle of Man has suffered...from the excess of its own popularity. For many years past it has been the favourite touring ground of holiday-makers from the crowded manufacturing district of South Lancashire and this perhaps has rather tended to discourage those quiet lovers of Nature who...do not always appreciate the joys of a noisy crowd...'* He went on to describe how Douglas, Ramsey, Port Erin and Peel *'are centres from which brakes and char-a-bancs and waggonettes perambulate every corner of the Island; even the culminating summit of Snaefell itself is now climbed by a double line of electric railway and crowned by a huge hotel. There is scarcely a glen in the whole island that is not rigorously kept under lock and key, and only to be opened at a price. Most people who love Nature will avoid Mona in the 'season' but luckily the 'season' is short. From October to Easter the lodging houses are empty and the island lives its own peculiar life.'* [1]

In 1913 the Island's entertainment scene was so buoyant that the Villa Marina concert venue opened to huge fanfare, in anticipation of another vibrant season.

But even in the Isle of Man it was hard to ignore the black clouds building on the horizon and when the First World War broke out at the height of the season in August 1914 visitor numbers plummeted. The Steam Packet had a fleet of fifteen vessels at that time and the requisition of ships by the Admiralty meant transport across the Irish Sea suddenly became severely restricted.

During the war, Cunningham's Camp, previously a hugely popular men-only holiday camp, was converted into an Internment Camp for Enemy Aliens. Likewise, Knockaloe farm on the Island's west coast soon became a high-security home to thousands of unwelcome visitors, mainly Germans and Austrians, whose presence aroused suspicion and fear among the local population.

The Great War brought devastation for many Manx families who lost fathers, brothers, sons and uncles. From Laxey the war claimed forty-one lives, their names listed in a roll of honour in the Valley Gardens.

War and Industry

Scarcity of labour was the main factor determining the shape of the Manx economy from 1900 to 1920. With the onset of war hundreds of men between the ages of 18 and 41 volunteered for military service and the visiting industry that had transformed the Island's labour scene evaporated virtually overnight. Young women could no longer rely on tourism-related jobs for an income and in response a private philanthropist set up the Manx Industries Association Ltd, providing employment for 250 women and girls making socks, mittens, mufflers and overcoats for the troops[2].

The difficult labour situation seriously affected the Island's textile industries. The manufacture of woollen cloths and blankets, hemp ropes, cotton and herring nets were now all in decline, unable to compete with larger, more organized manufactories elsewhere. In 1901 520 people were employed in Manx textile fabric manufacture but by 1911 this had dropped to 390[3] and stayed at that level until after the war.

During the actual war years certain occupations of 'national importance' allowed employees to become exempt from military service. In 1916 the British and Manx governments issued lists of these reserved occupations, mostly relating to agricultural work to ensure continuation of essential food supplies. The war also had direct repercussions for the Laxey mines. The mine workings had been in steady decline since the late nineteenth century and many miners had left the Island to seek their fortunes in America, South Africa and the Antipodes. But the First World War brought a new demand for metals and those mineworkers left behind were suddenly needed. This gave them the chance to seek better pay and working conditions and union militancy gained new strength. In 1917 a Laxey branch of the Worker's Union was formed and on the 20th April 1918 employees of the Great Laxey Mine came out on strike after directors refused to increase their wages. Their militancy was short-lived, though, and the Minister of Munitions ordered them to return to work pending a decision on the matter [4]. By 1920 the price of metal had once again dropped, little ore was being extracted and periods of inactivity had led to rising water levels underground. The mine's heyday was over.

Life in Laxey

'Laxey opens out as suddenly as Nice opens out to those who turn the corner of the hill on the road down from Villefranche and Beaulieu. This large and prosperous village – it is really a little town – occupies a situation entirely different from any other settlement in the island – it is rather like that of Lynmouth – on the short strath where two glens commingle before their united waters run out into the sea' [5].

In 1900 Laxey and Lonan had a population of around two and a half thousand people and by 1911 only two hundred of these were miners. Fortunately for Laxey businesses though, the district's green and pleasant attractions could still be relied on to pull in the crowds.

Once the Glen Gardens were acquired by the Manx Electric Railway they introduced military bands for regular summer concerts and these proved hugely popular. Every year the trams brought hundreds of thousands of visitors to the village and up until the First World War the gardens were vibrant and busy, with an ornate gated entrance leading into carefully tended parklands, a smart restaurant with dozens of tables laid with white linen and an outdoor dance floor filled with happy couples. Unfortunately, at the height of the 1913 season the ornate wooden Pavillion was devastated by fire, causing thousands of pounds worth of damage.

Laxey Glen Gardens

'The Beauty Spot of Mona, Laxey Glen Gardens, by electric tram or horse car to the gates. Dinner, luncheons, teas, cake and wine. Cycling, boating, shooting, bowling, billiards, tennis, croquet, strawberries and cream, music and dancing.'
Mona's Herald 27th June 1900

Listening to the band in Laxey Glen Gardens

Band, Laxey Glen Gardens, I. O. M.

Despite this incident, however, visitors to Laxey were unlikely to go hungry. The road to the Big Wheel was lined with small terraced houses which opened their doors for hearty food such as roast dinners, ham, eggs, tea and generous puddings, giving the road its alternative name of 'Ham and Egg Terrace'.

Up at the Big Wheel itself there was also a very popular Café and Boarding House which did a roaring trade, seating up to 150 people. On the corner opposite Dumbell's Terrace, Shepherd's café (later the Avondale), with its verandah and silver service, offered smart lunches and teas; and down on the promenade visitors could enjoy seaside refreshments at the Wavecrest café, originally run by the MacCormack family from a tin-roofed hut.

Entrance to Laxey Glen Gardens

Edwardian visitors could now, thrillingly, record their trip to Laxey with photographs. The village had a number of professional photographers such as Noah Spence Lees and John Kelly who had booths at strategic locations around the village where holidaymakers could pose against a painted backdrop of the Wheel or other attractions.

For Laxey's residents daily life was also changing. People could now communicate with each other via a new-fangled contraption called 'the telephone' – by July 1906 five Laxey people had a telephone number, plus there was a 'public call office' on New Road.

On the roads it was sometimes possible to see the occasional motor car go by in a flurry of mud or dust. In 1912 the only person in Laxey with a registered private vehicle (out of just 260 on the whole island) was W. H. Jane who owned a 9hp Riley. The local general practitioner Dr Godson owned a Douglas motorcycle[6]. By 1914 a local business was even the proud owner of a steam lorry.

Photograph taken in Laxey photo booth c. 1910

Domestic services were also improving. Gas and oil lighting were gradually being replaced by electricity and water supplies had improved to such an extent that villagers now paid water rates. New sewerage pipes were being laid along the Glen Road and, aided by the slowing of the mine works, the river was gradually returning to life. Ash pits and closets were still in use by poorer families though and despite advances in sanitation and medicine death records from this period make sombre reading, the majority of Laxey's population dying an 'unnatural' death as a result of accident or disease. Poverty was by no means unknown and the poorest families in the neighbourhood often had to rely on community fund-raising or Rechabite societies or, if things got really tough, admission to the Home for the Poor in Douglas[7] but this must have been a degrading and terrible last resort.

Laxey School c. 1900, including the son of woollen weaver James Moore of Minorca (back row, 3rd from left)

Children were now expected to attend school from an early age and the small but busy Glen Road Infant School opposite the St George's Woollen Mill was open right through these years and educated many of the children of mill workers. Children also worked part-time outside school hours, helping with farming, fishing and domestic chores, but there was still plenty of fun to be had, with the usual church gatherings, festivals, sports and district fairs in May and August.

Residents certainly had no call to leave the village for their daily requirements. Retailing in both New and Old Laxey was all go, with grocery suppliers, bakeries, newsagents, pie shops, butchers and clothing outfitters doing a good trade.

Edwardian Dress

'T.A. Mylroie's Drapery for all the latest fashions with ladies' costumes made-to-measure'.
1918 IOM Examiner Annual

Everyone wore wool during this period but many domestic manufacturers were struggling to compete with large scale imports of European made cloth. This situation temporarily abated when an Act was passed in 1916 prohibiting the importation into the Island of woollen goods manufactured outside the UK[9]. But in 1910 the woollen industry had been dealt a blow that was to have far-reaching consequences. Rayon, the world's first artificial fibre, was introduced and the history of clothing took a dramatic new turn. Rayon was made from wood pulp and its arrival signalled a revolution in the manufacture of fabric.

Wool still had a myriad of uses, however, for both sexes and all ages. Light weight cloth was used for occasion wear such as weddings; heavier or 'hard wear' fabric was used for everyday and country wear. Sportswear was increasingly popular and extended to cricket, golf, croquet and rowing. Although men's everyday garments remained little changed from the Victorian era they were influenced by the flamboyant Prince of Wales, a stickler for proper dress. His love of outdoor pursuits certainly increased the popularity of tweed, Homburg hats and Norfolk jackets and his preference for black evening dress was instrumental in the change from the traditional white.

A typical gentleman's wardrobe was likely to include a single-breasted morning coat made of black or dark grey wool serge with a waistcoat and striped 'spongebag' woollen serge trousers. Older men wore frock coats which were double-breasted and knee length, again in dark grey or black wool. Both these items were gradually replaced by the lounge jacket which was double-breasted with short lapels and curving front panels. For added insulation men could wear a close-fitting, one-piece woollen underwear garment called a 'union suit'. This later developed into the two-piece underwear items known as 'long johns.'

Working clothes for men and boys were still based around the single-breasted jacket with narrow lapels, woollen trousers or knee-length breeches, caps and flannel shirts. In the Manx countryside the rural dress of a typical farmer remained fairly simple *'He is clad in homespun woollen cloth or 'kialter', coloured 'keeir' or grey from the undyed fleece of the laughtyn or native sheep.'* [10]

Women's fashions, meanwhile, were undergoing a minor revolution. By the 1900s curved, flowing lines were becoming popular and more delicate colours were being introduced. The word 'costume' was applied to female clothing in this era - specifically a tailor-made suit, comprising a long skirt and jacket, often made of fine or 'artistic' woollen serge. Tailored suits were well established by

"The home industries once carried on in farmhouse and cottage, in the carding and spinning of flax and wool, and the weaving of linen, flannel and homespun cloth have quite disappeared. The spinning wheel is no longer found, except as an ornament in the drawing rooms of the wealthy; and even the knitting of stockings is no longer a cottage industry. …the country weaver with a loom or two in his cottage, once found in every district, has entirely disappeared." [8]
'The Isle of Man' Rev John Quine, 1911

1900 and marked the increasing independence of women. They were particularly useful garments for women in the workplace such as teachers and secretaries.

Visitors on the summit of Snaefell, c. 1910

Woollen skirts were still long but now gored, or panelled, making them less bulky and more flattering to the artificially slim Edwardian figure, nipped at the waist by tight corsets. Jackets were produced in a huge variety of styles, mostly short but with endless variations on sleeves, lapels and tailoring. For women able to enjoy motoring in a public passenger vehicle the woollen muffler or neck warmer was vital, as was the long dustcoat or 'duster' which quite literally protected the wearer from flying dust and oil specks. The cape was a huge fashion item in the first years of the twentieth century for similar reasons, giving much needed protection from inclement weather. Capes and mantles came in a range of styles, usually with practical high collars, but were gradually refined into less bulky coats.

The boating lake in Laxey Glen Gardens, c. 1910

Postcards advertising the Laxey Glen Gardens showed a range of contemporary fashions – ladies in long, ankle length skirts, blouses and fitted jackets, men smartly attired in three-piece suits, young boys in dark wool suits splashing on the boating lake and bowlers in shirt-sleeves and waistcoats. And absolutely everyone wore hats…

Edwardian swimsuits were similar to Victorian styles, made of wool and consisting of bloomers and an overdress. The dress was now sleeveless though and the outfit was worn with black stockings and laced footwear. By 1920 necklines were lowered further and the overdress shortened even more.

Rural Manx women didn't have quite so much variety, still stuck in their uniform of linsey-woolsey petticoat and 'loose jacket with a broad collar, called the 'bedgown', drawn in at the waist by a linen apron'[11]. The Manx blanket shawl existed in country areas until at least the end of the First World War.

Colour was increasingly employed in the manufacture of smart, expensive clothing with a new fashion for delicate shades such as rose pink, eau-de-nil and pale blue but these were generally applied to fine fabrics and trimmings. Woollen cloth largely remained dark, monochromatic and drab. Synthetic dyes were now accepted alongside the old favourites such as indigo and logwood but in the early part of the century only a tiny percentage of material brought into the Laxey mill to be dyed was anything other than black or navy blue.

However, the dye market changed dramatically with the outbreak of World War One. Germany was the main producer and exporter of commercial dyes and when their dye factories switched to making explosives the resulting dye shortage quickly drove prices up and a number of American dye companies were established to fill the gap[12].

Aside from clothing, wool was still used extensively around the home. Woollen blankets were in great demand and a material called 'Manx sheeting'[13] provided a useful cross between a sheet and a blanket. This was made with a cotton warp and a wool weft, similar to the earlier linsey-woolsey.

'T.J.Halsall of New Road, Laxey for men's suits, overcoats and rainproofs, tailoring costumes a speciality'.
1918 IOM Examiner Annual

The Men From Huddersfield

As the new century dawned the Laxey Mill was still in the hands of Egbert Rydings, now in his late Sixties, and James Forster, who had been promoted from weaver to mill manager. Despite Egbert's personal reservations about the success of the venture local commentators considered that 'the fabrics turned out by Mr Rydings' mill have achieved world-wide celebrity for beauty and durability'[14]. But it had been a long haul and when he was approached in 1901 by a successful Yorkshire woollen merchant he decided it was time to hand over the reins. Later that year George Holroyd and his son Frederic took out a ten year lease on the mill and Egbert was finally able to retire.

The Holroyds were from Huddersfield, one of England's largest

George Holroyd c. 1907

textile towns, and had a long family history as cloth manufacturers and merchants. George was born in 1851 and by the age of thirty was managing a worsted mill in Yorkshire. He then set up as a self-employed woollen dealer in Huddersfield in a district where every family was involved in the woollen industry – as weavers, serge weavers, balers and woollen manufacturers. At the time the Holroyds took over the Laxey mill George's eldest son Frederic, or Freddie as he was known, was aged just 24 and himself the manager of a worsted factory. Although George renamed the Laxey enterprise 'Geo. Holroyd & Son' this may have been in name only as he continued to run a successful woollen cloth mill in Station Street, Huddersfield and it was actually Freddie who ran the Manx enterprise. There was also another son, Herman, who ran a similar business in Radnorshire but he was killed on military service in 1918.

Frederic Holroyd c. 1907

For the first few years of the takeover the Laxey Mill continued to be managed by James Forster but when he died in 1906 the day-to-day running of the mill was taken over by young Freddie and within six months local newspapers were noting how 'they have been enterprising and today Ruskin Home Spuns are doing an increasing business, not only throughout the United Kingdom, but there is seldom a post which does not bring orders from the Colonies, America and other foreign countries'[15]. The new men at the helm were an 'expert publicity machine' and they not only sent out regular trade newsletters but ensured the mill was advertised in the likes of Punch, The Fishing Gazette and Tatler magazines[16].

'The goods manufactured at the St George's Mill include All-wool Dress Cloths, Costume Cloths, Men's Suitings and Trouserings, pure Wool Blankets, flannels, stockings, travelling rugs, knitting yarn etc. Suits and costumes are made up to customers own measure and self-measurement forms are supplied. Among the specialities are Ruskin Homespuns and artistic serges. In colour and texture they are extremely fine; they are non-shrinkable and non-fading. For these and other reasons they rank among the finest dress fabrics for ladies; and the homespuns are made in heavier grades for men's wear. Patterns and particulars will be sent post free to any address on receipt of a postcard addressed to G. Holroyd & Son, St George's Mill, Laxey, Isle of Man. Most Manx drapers and tailors either stock the Ruskin Manx Homespun goods or list the patterns.'
Manx Patriot Jan 1907 Vol. 1, No.4

Freddie was a little man, quick and sharp and well-liked. Like his predecessor he was keen to become involved in the community and served his first term as a Laxey Commissioner in 1912, remaining on the board continuously for the next ten years. He was also a stalwart of the local football club. He was financially astute and resided in some of the villages finest houses – 'Eden Vale' (since demolished) on the Glen Road, 'Ellan Vannin House' and a large, Victorian mansion known as Bramble Brae (now 'Cooil Ard'). Freddie's wife Annis was also well-known in the community, mainly for her fine soprano singing voice which had served her well in the Huddersfield Choral Society. One Laxey resident recalls her boasting that "she had so many certificaytes (as she pronounced it) for singing that she didn't have room for them all on the wall"!... In Laxey she conducted the choir of the Glen Road Methodist church and was a key player at Laxey Choral Society and Primitive Methodist concerts[17]. Freddie and Annis had two sons, Leonard and Arthur.

Once their ten year lease on the mill expired the Holroyds were still keen to progress the business. In November 1911, when Egbert and his co-owners put the mill up for auction, the entire property, land, plant and machinery was sold to Thomas Taylor of Leeds, acting as the Holroyds' agent. Three months later, he conveyed the property to the Holroyds[18]. The initial sale wasn't a deal that made Egbert rich. For his part of the sale he came away with just £137 and ten shillings. But for the Holroyds their commitment to the mill was soon justified. In 1913 the Laxey Mill received an order from King George V for Manx Ruskin Homespun cloth[19].

The Death of A Gentleman

Just a few months after the sale of his beloved mill, Egbert Rydings died quietly at home. It was the 12th April 1912 and he was eighty years old. The Lonan Death Register records his status as 'a gentleman'; the cause of his death 'senile decay, paraplegia and exhaustion'[20]. Not that the latter was surprising in a man who had always found it hard to sit still. Even into his seventies, he was pursuing his interests in the community, serving on the board of the South Cape School amongst other things.

On his death the Isle of Man Weekly Times was quick to pay tribute to a man considered as 'more Manx than the Manx people', 'a writer of more than average

'A man of considerable intellectual power and strong literary tastes...had he lived in a different environment he would probably have figured more largely in the literary world for he had a deep insight into character and great natural humour.'
Obituary for Egbert Rydings
IOM Weekly Times April
20th 1912

ability' who 'represented in a remarkable manner in his own personality the close relations which have always obtained between the peoples of Lancashire and the Isle of Man'. The newspaper also praised him as 'an enthusiastic upholder of the Ruskin gospel of sincerity and nobleness and its practical development on the lines of honest craftsmanship as opposed to shoddy and shabby' [21].

The mill 'experiment' may not have succeeded in quite the way Rydings and Ruskin originally envisaged, but the real success story in terms of Ruskin's teachings was probably Egbert himself - a working man who taught himself and others to appreciate the value of craftsmanship and the countryside; a talented writer who wrote about 'real life', a man who loved music and the arts and was deeply involved in his local community but above all, tried to better the lot of the working people around him. And all because he was inspired by the writings of John Ruskin.

Egbert Rydings' headstone in Lonan churchyard

Egbert was laid to rest in Lonan churchyard with his first wife Eleanor.

Factory Life

Working conditions in the mill were subject to new scrutiny from the early 1900s. As part of an amended Factory and Workshops Act inspectors visited the mill at least once a year and reported their findings to the Manx Government, including the number of industrial accidents recorded on site.

The actual manufactory leased by the Holroyds in 1901 was a substantial, virtually self-sufficient property. Surrounding the main building there were outhouses, drying sheds, a 'large power water wheel' and land to the rear and side. Inside the factory itself there was machinery for cleaning, spinning and weaving the wool. During their first decade of operation the Holroyds also bought in new finishing machines to carry out the job formerly done by local fulling mills. Here, once again, the experience of the Forster family came into its own. James Forster's older sister Ann had been the fuller at the Bowring Mill so he would have been familiar with the processes and equipment involved. His son John, employed at the Mill as a weaver and dyer, now added 'finisher' to his job description.

The Holroyd workforce expanded considerably in their first ten years, numbering up to thirty employees when in full production [22]. Other key workers in these early years included James' younger son Tom Forster, who continued as a weaver in the Laxey Mill until his retirement. The mill's main dyer Margaret Kewley also continued to work there well into old age.

In 1907 the mill's production methods were praised in an advertorial in the Manx Patriot as 'a harking back to the times of our grandfathers when the tricks and devices of cheapening manufactured goods by all sorts of shoddy methods were unknown – the manufacture, under improved conditions, and at prices to compete with present day goods, of the class of fabrics once turned out from the hand loom. The Ruskin Home Spuns have only one drawback – they wear out very slowly' [23].

Farmers from all over the Island still brought their wool direct to the mill – giving rise to the later advertising slogan 'From Mountain Track to Wearer's Back' – and up until the middle of the First World War female employees sorted the wool and washed it by hand. But in 1917 Freddie Holroyd had a long, low stone building constructed on the left hand side of the main gates called a 'willeying' house (now offices). Here, in a move designed to save precious labour, the raw fleeces could be cleaned by machine.

After drying the wool was taken into the main factory and passed through two machines known as a Teaser and a Scribbler, the object being to open out the fibres of the wool (similar to carding). It was then passed over a condenser and came out in small rolls on bobbins ready for carrying to the spinning mule. After spinning it was taken up to the twisting frame where girls would literally twist single threads into two and three ply yarns to be used for stocking wool, shawls or cloth. Other processes known as warping, beaming and winding then took place and finally the actual process of weaving could begin. All the power for this machinery, and the mill's electricity, still came from a dynamo worked by the water-wheel. During the war years when coal and gas supplies became severely restricted, the ability to generate power through water was particularly advantageous.

The final process of finishing, previously known as fulling, was now done 'in-house'. Firstly the cloth was 'milled' to interlock the fibres followed by the usual scouring to clean, strengthen and shrink the material. This was repeated at least

Did you know?

Sheep which are less stressed are thought to produce better wool, so Manx wool is generally regarded as good quality.

four times then the finished cloth was put through a hydro-extractor (a machine that sucked out the water) or taken outside to be dried and bleached in the fresh air. The fuller's earth used at the mill probably still came from the Manx mine at Glen Wyllin which was taken over in 1903 by a Lancashire man, A.E.Grundy. His Glen Wyllin Fuller's Earth Company Ltd. was highly productive for a time, especially during the First World War when it was discovered that fuller's earth was also useful in the manufacture of shell cases. The mine eventually closed in 1919.

Advertising

The Holroyds may have had no direct connection with the Guild of St George or John Ruskin, but nevertheless made no bones about using his name and philosophies to sell their products. At around the time they purchased the mill they produced a pamphlet entitled 'Honest Cloth' which included a potted account of the mill's background and Ruskin's four 'rules' for honest trade.

'The goods made are :-

All-wool dress cloths	Pure wool blankets
Costume cloths	Flannels
Men's Suitings	Stockings
Men's Trouserings	Travelling Rugs
Knitting Yarns	

The specialities are Ruskin Homespuns and Artistic serges.

All the goods will be found of good quality. The cloths will not shrink or fade. The Ruskin Homespuns wear especially well and by reason of their beauty of make, color (sic), texture, fastness of dye and unshrinkableness are considered to be among the finest lady's dress fabrics made. Heavier homespuns are made for men's wear. A full set of patterns will be sent on receipt of postcard.'
'Honest Cloth' Pamphlet produced by the Holroyds, circa 1910-15, St George's Guild Archive, Sheffield

This pamphlet was used as the basis for a local advertising campaign in the annual Isle of Man Examiner Yearbooks which ran for several years. At one stage Freddie even embellished it with the idea that 'Ruskin lived at Laxey for some time...' This probably came from his knowledge of a house in the locality called Ruskinville which was variously said to have been owned or stayed in by the Master though neither was, in fact, true.

By 1914 the advert was tweaked again, this time emphasising their manufacture of 'ladies and gentlemen's hard wear' such as coats and mantles, but also asking readers to 'support Manx industries'[24].

Celebrity friends of the mill also continued to do their bit in publicising its good name. In Hall Caine's book on the Isle of Man published in 1909 he noted that 'Manx homespuns have a reputation which even the island of Harris might envy. A visit should be made therefore to the St George's Woollen Mills'[25].

At this time it was common practice for manufacturers to conduct guided tours of their works. Egbert Rydings was often quoted as doing it and Freddie Holroyd carried on the practice – "During a recent visit to Laxey we were conducted through the Mill by Mr Frederic Holroyd and saw the operation from start to finish"[26].

The End of Guild Involvement

The Mill's direct connections with the Guild of St George ended in 1901 with the retirement of Egbert Rydings but he remained enthusiastic in his promotion of Ruskin's Manx venture. Later that year he attended his last Guild meeting in Liverpool. This was an urgent crisis meeting called to decide whether the Guild should carry on or not in the light of Ruskin's death. The morning after the meeting Egbert had an informal get-together with his fellow Companions and regaled them with 'an informative talk' on the Manx woollen industry[27].

Despite the anxieties of many Companions the Guild did survive, and does so to this day, but once the Holroyds took over the mill any active support from the Guild came to an end and all outstanding mortgages and loans were fully paid off. John Ruskin's name was used in advertising right up to the Fifties but as he gradually faded in the public consciousness this was eventually dropped.

Embellished engraving of Rydings' original sketch with Ruskin's inscription. Note the addition of fishermen

First achievement of the St George's Company in Romantic architecture . . . J.R. 10th July 1881.

St. George's Mill, Laxey, Isle of Man (with facsimile of Mr. Ruskin's Inscription)

References:
1. 'The Isle of Man, Beautiful Britain' Joseph Morris, Adam & Black, London 1911 p.6
2. Manx Year Book 1916, Norris-Meyer Press, MNH
3. Manx Year Book 1914, Norris-Meyer Press, MNH
4. 'The Great Laxey Mine' Andrew Scarffe, Manx Heritage Foundation, 2004
5. Joseph Morris, ibid pp.44-45
6. Manx Year Book 1912 Norris-Meyer Press, MNH
7. 1910-1916 Minute Book of Lonan Poor Law Guardians, MNH
8. 'The Isle of Man' Rev John Quine, reprinted in Cambridge County Geographies ed. F.H.H. Guillemand, Camb University Press 1911
9. IOM Government circular No.191, Tynwald Library
10. 'Manx Yarns' A.E. LaMothe, Manx Sun 1905, MNH
11. Ibid
12. www.colourantshistory.org
13. 'Handloom Weavers in the North' Ralph Howarth, Presidential Address, IOMNHAS April 1939, MNH
14. IOM Examiner Annual 1902, Norris Meyer Press, MNH
15. Manx Patriot, Jan 1907 Vol.1, No.4 MNH
16. Hall Caine, letter to IOM Weekly Times Aug 11 1923 MNH
17. IOM Examiner, April 1911, MNH
18. ibid p.18
19. IOM Examiner Annual 1913 p.15, MNH
20. Egbert Rydings Death certificate B253, IOM Government Civil Registry
21. IOM Weekly Times, Saturday 20th April 1912, MNH
22. IOM Weekly Times 25th Nov, 1911 p.9, MNH
23. Manx Patriot, Jan 1907 Vol.1, No.4 MNH
24. Manx Year Book 1914 p.48, MNH
25. 'The Isle of Man' Hall Caine, Adam & Charles Black 1909, pp.139-140
26. Manx Patriot Jan 1907 Vol.1, No.4 MNH
27. Account of meeting of St George's Guild, Liverpool, 28th October 1901, Ruskin Library, Lancaster University

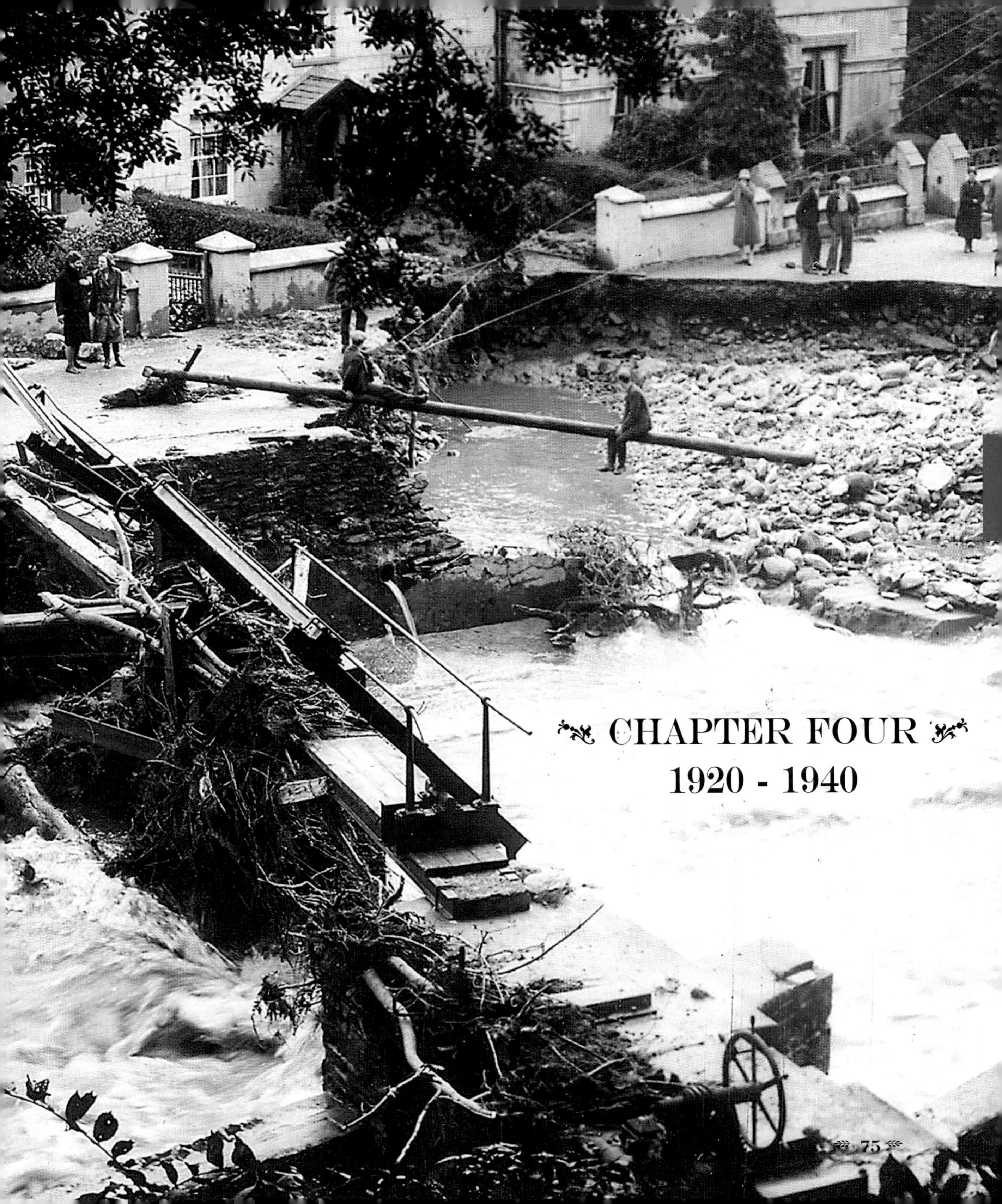

CHAPTER FOUR
1920 - 1940

Timeline

1920   Visit to the Isle of Man by King George V and Queen Mary

1921   Major fire at the Laxey Glen Flour Mills

1922   Moving pictures shown twice weekly at the Laxey Working Men's Institute

1922   Robert Williamson purchased the Great Laxey Mine

1923   New public tennis court and bowling green opened on Glen Road

1923   The Old Laxey Equitable Co-operative Society (the 'Down-Co') dissolved

1923   The St George's Mill Company Ltd. established by Egbert Rydings dissolved

1927   Death of influential Laxey businessman Robert Williamson

1929   New elementary school opened on Minorca Hill, replacing the National School (Laxey Mixed), Laxey Infants and South Cape schools

1929   Great Laxey Mine closed for the last time

1930   Laxey Tram Car Depot destroyed by fire

1930   Outbreak of scarlet fever in Laxey

1930   Heavy rain caused the Laxey river to burst its banks, flooding Glen Road

1932   Construction of Laxey promenade and sea wall

1932   Ballagawne School closed

1936   Death of King George V. Accession and abdication of Edward VIII

1936   Acquisition of Ballacregga reservoir, finally assuring reliable water supplies for Laxey

1936   Severe January snow affecting village school and businesses

1936   Measles outbreak caused closure of school for two weeks

1937   Coronation of King George VI. Village celebrations held

1939   Commencement of World War Two

1940   Nearly 13,000 tons of stone from the Laxey 'Deads' sold to Douglas Corporation

Peace Time

Between the wars the Isle of Man once again became a busy holiday destination. Remarkably, within just one year of the end of the First World war, the Island played host to over three hundred thousand visitors in a single season[1] and in 1920 numbers tipped the half million mark. For the next two decades the lure of sandy beaches, dance halls and tram rides brought a continual stream of happy holidaymakers to Manx shores. On one particularly memorable day in August 1937 more than sixty-eight thousand people were ferried to and from the Island in fifty separate sailings![2]

At this time the Steam Packet serviced more than half a dozen destination ports around the Irish Sea and a typical return rail-and-sail ticket from London to Douglas cost just three pounds[3]. The level of service was nevertheless incredibly high. The ships were attractive and comfortable, especially for first-class passengers who could relax in well-appointed cabins. And it didn't end there. If your steamer arrived in Ramsey you could hop straight onto a connecting electric tram car with luggage van attached and journey on to Laxey or Douglas. You didn't even have to handle your suitcase or trunk. All luggage could be sent straight through to the Laxey or Ramsey station from any British Rail Station and vice versa[4].

By the end of the Twenties the Isle of Man Publicity Board was keen to promote the Island as the place for a 'cheery, novel, bracing holiday'. Young men and families battered by the war were tempted with uplifting words such as 'jolly' and 'joy', and it wasn't long before the 'Douglas Bay New Holiday Camp for Men' was advertising its attractions. The Board was also keen to emphasise that the Island was no longer just a destination for workers from England's industrial northwest.

The Station Hotel on Snaefell Mountain summit

Sir John Foster Fraser, in his introduction to the 1929 Isle of Man Guide, says he expected to see 'multitudes of noisy trippers wearing shawls and clattering clogs' but in fact met lots of 'genial Yorkshire and Lancashire folk...plenty of Irish people, people from the Midlands, from America and the Dominions, people from the south of England, who I believe are called 'country folk', and innumerable Londoners'[5].

Improved Island-wide transport certainly helped attract a wider range of visitor. Getting around was now so much easier and more comfortable than in the days of horse and coach, with plenty of motoring on 400 miles of 'excellent' roads'. Once visitors were out and about they could visit 'out of the way hamlets where people who can speak the Manx tongue better than the English are to be found'[6].

In Douglas large-scale entertainment was still immensely popular. Huge crowds attended daily orchestral concerts at the Villa Marina; the beach teemed with people and thousands attended the weekly open air church service at Braddan. Plus, the Island was already being advertised as a mecca for motor-racing.

Unfortunately the revival of the visiting industry was not enough to restore the local economy to its pre-War levels. The Island had taken some heavy blows during the Great War, losing over a thousand men of working age and leaving many unable to work on their return. By the mid-1930s nearly two thousand Islanders were registered unemployed[7] and Manx agriculture was in the middle of an eight year depression.

Laxey in the Twenties

Axnfell Hostel and Guest House. A popular Laxey restorative retreat

The 1920s opened on a thrilling note for the residents of Laxey when, on the 15th July, the village received a visit from King George V and Queen Mary. Up to four hundred schoolchildren lined the sides of New Road from the Glen Hotel to the Queen's Hotel to wave to their Majesties as they drove along in a royal convoy[8].

For many Laxey families though, such special days were few and far between. Life between the wars was hard, especially for those who had relied on an income from the failing mines or the Flour Mill which, a year after the royal visit, suffered a major fire that left many workers unemployed. Food and new clothing were difficult to come by and many children still went about barefoot. Fund-raising entertainments were even held in the Working Men's Institute to subsidise the Poor Relief available to particularly hard-up families.

Not that village youngsters allowed such austerity to get in the way of having fun. Aside from the free entertainment to be had on the open sands and rocks of the main beach there was plenty of adventure to be had exploring the banks of the

Laxey river. The water was starting to return to normal and a small sandy 'beach' that had formed halfway down Glen Road made a natural gathering place. Healthy fish stocks were increasing and both river and sea fishing were popular pastimes. Young boys could also make a pretty penny selling buckets of freshly caught mackerel and gibbins dug from the sand.

In 1929, following the closure of the National School on Ramsey Road, all primary school children were expected to attend the brand new Laxey Elementary school on Minorca Hill. The Infants school, just over the river from the woollen mills, closed its doors shortly afterwards[9].

By the mid-1920s many villagers could enjoy the benefits of electricity supplied by the Douglas generating station. In 1929 the Laxey Electric Light and Power Company Ltd was established but, even then, many public buildings such as the working men's institutes were not supplied with electricity until the Thirties. They were still able to offer a multitude of entertainments, though. The Old Laxey Reading Room regularly held socials, concerts and tombolas alongside their billiard tables and library, and members could use the well-equipped gymnasium on the top floor of the adjacent Warehouse. Which they may well have needed - the teas held at the Reading Room were legendary, on one occasion providing 40 pounds of bunloaf and 20 pounds of seed loaf![10]

Dinner

'Best one shilling dinners on the Island. Pure lamb and beef with green peas, cabbage or beans, potatoes, mint sauce and bread – Miss Cowin's, 11 & 12 Dumbell's Terrace, Laxey Guide

Laxey Harbour, I.O.M.

Laxey Harbour. The Warehouse and Reading Room are on the left

The village itself was still widely scattered between a collection of small hamlets each with their own shopping area. Grocery deliveries were sent round Lower Laxey by the 'Down Co', which had an adjoining bakery and coalhouse, but this went into liquidation in 1923 (Freddie Holroyd was actually one of the liquidators).

In Upper Laxey the 'Upper Co' continued to do a roaring trade, providing just about everything under the sun. At this time it was a two storey affair with individual areas selling shoes, clothing, drapery, hardware, food, household utensils, coal, homemade bakery items and meat pies. The meat was as local as it could be – having been slaughtered just down the road on Glen Road. Goods were wrapped in paper and when customers paid for their items their money was sent to the cash desk on a 'zip wire'.

Once you had done your shopping you could sit awhile in the nearby rose gardens – where the flowers bloomed especially well thanks to the human waste collected from local residents by the Commissioner's cart!

The centre for most commerce in Laxey in the Twenties was the New Road, from the Post Office all the way up to the Queen's Hotel. Mr Kinrade's barbers, Tate's paper and sweet shop, Mylroie's drapery run by the ever dapper Mr Mylroie,

LAXEY VILLAGE. NEW ROAD.

Shopping in New Road, Laxey

Dibbs' grocery shop, the Corlett sisters' fruit and vegetable shop, Williamson's emporium, Ma Kennaugh's sweet shop, Miss Cowley's milliners, and many other small businesses provided a range of specialist services.

Residents, used to being able to walk in the road without fear of accident, now had to look both ways as the advent of the motor car and omnibus opened the village up as the perfect destination for a day out. In the late 1920s public bus services started servicing Laxey with regular rides to Douglas. Each of the three main bus companies were distinguished by the colour of their vehicles. Manxland's were red, Manx Motors a grey-green colour and Isle of Man Road Services, blue. After dark the buses were simply distinguished by the colour of their lights. Village roads were still largely unsealed until the Thirties, however, so bus travel may have seemed glamorous but was likely to be a little bumpy.

Daily employment in Thirties Laxey largely revolved around farming and small local businesses, including retailing and hospitality, but there were some larger industries. The Glen Flour Mill was back in business and the Erskine Clothing Company on the quay and St George's Woollen Mill were major employers. Textile manufacture in the Lonan district also extended to an industrial product called bratticecloth. This was a fire resistant cloth hung in mine tunnels as a fire break.

'My father was a miner in the Snaefell Mines. We lived in a small cottage on the riverside of Glen Road. Grocery and newsagents' shops were plentiful. Phil Betton ran a very popular fish 'n chip shop on Glen Road (now the launderette) and the Co-op had a coal house near the football field. Milk deliveries came from Ballakiljolough in Bobby Clague's horse and cart. The milk was kept in highly polished churns with shiny brass plates. Every Sunday the Salvation Army Band went round the village, holding a service on the New Road by the Co-op and ending up in the hall on Shore Road (now the nursery) where local people would bring fruit and veg to auction off for a Harvest Home.'
(1930s Reminiscences of Bernard Cowley of Glen Road, Laxey)

The Big Flood

In September 1930 Laxey made headlines – but for all the wrong reasons. A torrential downpour of rain lasting over eight hours swept over the whole Island and in Laxey the force of the water burst the weir in the river running alongside Glen Road. Many properties were severely flooded, bridges were swept away and the river deposited over four thousand tons of rubble in its wake. Even the Woollen Mills, though slightly above the flood level, was still affected with water entering the ground floor. Some residents lost all their belongings and furniture and, as these were days before insurance was usual practice, the devastation was deeply felt. The destruction even prompted a visit by the Island's Lieutenant Governor who launched a distress fund[11].

Glen Road resident Bernard Cowley vividly remembers the flood. He was just nine years old at the time and lived in a row of small cottages built for the miners called Cumberland Cottages (since demolished). A family of nine children lived in the tiny house next door. Within a short time Bernard's cottage was four feet deep in swirling water and mud but luckily a quick-thinking neighbour flung a rope across the swollen river and the family shimmied with bare feet to safety. Once on the other side they made their way up the 'brough' (hill) to take refuge with an Aunt who lived higher up.

The aftermath of the big flood. Laxey, September 1930

'A Room and A Welcome'

'Seven miles north of Douglas, and embosomed in a valley running down to the sea, is Laxey, a village once dependent on its lead and silver mines... The angler and the walker who prefer rambling of the strenuous kind will find all their wants supplied in this district...the streams in Glen Roy, Laxey Glen and at the Dhoon have a fair run of trout and the angler can apply his art amid sylvan surroundings. In Laxey Glen Gardens are tennis courts, an open-air dancing floor and croquet lawns, while children are catered for by swings, roundabouts, and a miniature boating lake. Good bathing, boating and sea fishing may be had in the sheltered bay.' (1929 IOM Guide)

Visitors did still come to Laxey in the 1920s but in nowhere near the numbers experienced in the late nineteenth and early twentieth centuries. The slow demise of the Laxey Mines, and their final closure in 1929, ended a major chapter in the district's history and development and meant not only the end of metal ore extraction as a source of income, but the end of the mine workings and washing floors as a visitor attraction. Observers noted that *'The leadmines...have not the importance that once was theirs. But they provide one of the 'sights' of Laxey'* [12]. By 1934 the Laxey Wheel was merely 'an attractive curiosity' [13].

The seaside also still had something of an industrial feel to it. Commercial boats plied a steady route across the bay bringing in grain and other supplies for local industry, and fuel supplies were brought in on three coal boats – the Ben Veg or 'Little Girl', Ben Varrey or 'Middle Girl' and the Ben Vooar 'Big Girl'. During the Twenties the beach had no formal promenade, just a long stretch of sand and sloping bank of pebbles bordered with grass, in the middle of which

A rather grim Laxey beach

stood a stone building used as a lead store for the mines (now a café and seating shelter). It wasn't until 1932 that the village commissioners realised the seafront's potential to attract greater numbers of visitors and approved the construction of a sea wall and paved promenade which gave the area an instant facelift.

A 1926 postcard advertising Laxey's natural charms!

In the meantime, the southern end of the bay provided a pleasant place to while away a sunny day. Here locals and visitors could enjoy swimming in the shallows and sunbathing on the rocks. The waters of Lord Henry's well, at one time believed to heal eye complaints, had long since dried up but were still acknowledged in the naming of the nearby 'Henry's Café'. On the adjacent green the local church held an annual outdoor service known as Hospital Sunday at which donations were collected for Noble's Hospital.

Up in the village visitors may no longer have been able to rely on the mines for entertainment but they quickly discovered that a cream tea and a wander in the Glen offered perfectly pleasant substitutes for industrial amusement. In 1934 A.G. Wilcox wrote in his book 'Pleasure Island', 'had a jolly day in Laxey having tea and cakes at the Glen Gardens then visiting a 'glorified snack bar' on Dumbell's Row'[14]. And, of course, there was always the excitement of a ride on the Mountain Railway tramcar to the top of Snaefell for spectacular views and a bite to eat at the Station Hotel.

One area in which Laxey could excel in the post-war era was as a restorative retreat. Accommodation was offered by numerous boarding-houses, apartments and farmhouses. At the Axnfell guest house high up on the southern slopes of

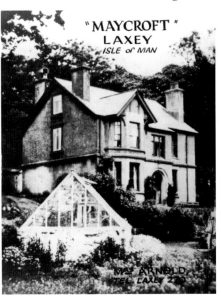

Laxey valley visitors could have their 'mental cobwebs blown away...amidst pine trees and larches'[15]. Or if you chose to stay closer to the heart of the village there were the comforts of the new Gardens Hotel, adjoining the famous Glen, with the added attraction of open-air music and dancing[16]. Visitors staying at the Maycroft Nursery Gardens in Old Laxey could take advantage of an abundance of fresh fruit and vegetables grown on the doorstep.

In the mid-1930s some bright spark in the tourism industry discovered that a particular type of seaweed found in abundance on Laxey beach was useful as a cure for rheumatoid arthritis. The idea was worked in to all local publicity and gave the area even more kudos 'as a desirable place to stay'[17].

> 'In Laxey they chant:
> Come in the evening,
> Come in the morning,
> Come when expected,
> Come without warning.
> A room and a welcome
> There's always for you,
> And the oftener you come
> The more we'll adore you!'[18]

As the Thirties went on the holiday guide writers became more and more poetic in their descriptions of Laxey, until by 1939 – in the vain hope the new war would be short-lived – it was being promoted as the place for 'Jolli-Olli-Days'.

Rising Hemlines

The appearance of women's ankles was probably the defining fashion trend of the post-First World War era. The war had changed many attitudes towards the role of the sexes and female legs were not only suddenly visible but were even occasionally seen clothed in trousers! The advent of movies also presented the public with screen idols from whom they could copy ideas. Greta Garbo, Marlene Dietrich, Katherine Hepburn, Rudolph Valentino and Clark Gable were all admired as much for their looks and dress as their acting skills and Dietrich and Hepburn lent new acceptability to women wearing trousers. By the mid-Thirties Manx women were even seen wearing colourful, bell-bottomed trousers – and occasionally markedly male plus-fours and polo sweaters.

The popular dancing floor at Laxey Glen Gardens

The excitement of rising hemlines was counteracted though by a new straight-up-and-down shapelessness that encapsulated female fashions in the Twenties and

Captain's Hill, Laxey, October 1935. The right-hand cottages known as Mylrea's Terrace were later demolished

Thirties. The androgynous look became fashionable for society belles, personified by the Flapper styles that relied on short haircuts and plenty of sparkle and feathers. But for ordinary, everyday wear this was not an era that flattered women. Laxey women were now confined to straight, dreary calf-length dresses worn with stockings, drab cardigans, shapeless hats and double breasted coats.

Working men and boys still wore woollen trousers, jackets and waistcoats and flat caps but for men-about-town the picture was considerably brighter. *'We males have suede shoes this season...shirts which vary in colour, with short-sleeves, loud check jackets...trousers which retain their braces...and coloured berets which we store in our hip pockets until required'* [19].

A dapper 1930's gent

Manx tweed was gaining itself a reputation abroad, particularly in the field of country pursuits.

As had been the case with King Edward VII, the changing line-up of royalty in the 1930s had a marked impact on clothing and fashions. Edward VIII was a smart, snappy dresser and even after his abdication he and his American wife Wallis Simpson were admired by fashionistas for their glamorous style. Once George VI took the throne with the much-loved Queen Mother, Elizabeth Bowes-Lyon, they introduced even more stylistic changes which the public followed with great avidity.

All Quiet at the Mill

The 1920s began on a sombre note for the 'Ruskin Mill'. On the 12th December 1921 George Holroyd passed away at the age of seventy, leaving the business in the hands of his oldest son Freddie. In 1923 the St George's Mill Company Ltd, established by Egbert Rydings, was dissolved and for the remainder of the period Freddie continued in sole occupation of the mill under the name Geo. Holroyd & Son. In 1924 he was even able to install the

Did you know?
A single woollen fibre is called a 'staple'.

factory's first telephone. The number wasn't hard to remember, being just a single digit – Laxey 8.

The Twenties were lean times for the Island's woollen manufacturing industries but Freddie had little local competition. The 1925 IOM Trade Directory lists only Holroyd's and Moores of Tynwald Mills as Woollen Manufacturers. Local rumour had it that Freddie 'bought more shoddy than wool' but as 'honesty' was the crux of his advertising it's unlikely he would have risked such practices and the rumours are likely to have been the result of a tough business climate.

Complete in-house production from start to finish was proudly promoted by the slogan 'From the mountain track to the wearer's back' painted on a placard and placed between two windows on the front of the mill. The range of products manufactured by Holroyd & Son changed little during this period and their biggest seller was still 'the celebrated Ruskin Homespuns'. Customers continued to buy direct from the mill and although there was a small wool shop in the village on the New Road, between Annie Williamson's sweet shop and Shepherd's Café (now Blacks Fireplaces), it's uncertain whether this shop belonged to the Holroyds.

Throughout the Twenties and Thirties Freddie also continued to take an active part in village affairs and in 1936 was once again serving on the local board of Commissioners. He seems to have been well-liked in the community and is remembered for thoughtful gestures. On hearing of the birth of a local resident's first son he asked her to call into the mill where he presented her with a pair of new woollen blankets (which lasted for many years afterwards!).

Little is known about the people working in the mill or day-to-day business during the inter-war years. No records survive from the period but one name that is remembered is that of Walter Titterington who lived across the river from the mill in a row of small white terraced cottages. Riverside Terrace (since demolished) was referred to locally as 'Rotten Row' but the families who lived there were known for their neighbourliness to one another. There were also two large cottages behind the mill and stables used by Kermode the Carter but these were later demolished.

In the late Thirties the mill's reliance on water power came to an end and in around 1937 the waterwheel that had powered the vision of John Ruskin and Egbert Rydings was dismantled for good.

Country clothes

'For country clothes there are now some very attractive homespuns and the very latest tweeds come from the Isle of Man and are known as Manx tweeds.'
(Vanity Fair 1923 [20])

References:
1. 1919 Manx Year Book, MNH
2. 'The Isle of Man – A Social, Cultural and Political History' R.H. Kinvig, 3rd Edition, Liverpool University Press 1975
3. 1929 IOM Guide, Isle of Man Publicity Board, intro
4. Manx Electric Railway advertisement, 1929 IOM Guide
5. ibid
6. 1929 IOM Guide intro
7. 'The Isle of Man – A Study In Economic Geography' J.W. Birch, Cambridge University Press 1964
8. Laxey Village Commissioners Minutes MS09797, MNH
9. 'Manx Schools, Past, Present and Proposed' Ronald S. Ely 2003
10. 1922 Old Laxey Reading Room minutes, private collection
11. 'Inner Mann' S. Dearden & K. Hassell, Stenlake Publishing 2003
12. 1930 Guide to The Isle of Man 'Pleasure Island', London Midland and Scottish Railway Company
13. 1934 Isle of Man Official Guide, Isle of Man Publicity Board p.14
14. 'Pleasure Island' A.G. Wilcox, Cunliffe Bros. 1934 p.242
15. Advertisement, 1929 IOM Guide p.111
16. ibid
17. 1934 Isle of Man Official Guide, Isle of Man Publicity Board
18. Wilcox, ibid p.242
19. Wilcox, ibid p.65
20. Vanity Fair, reprinted in IOM Weekly Times Aug 11 1923, MNH

LAXEY, ISLE OF MAN.   R.1794.

CHAPTER FIVE
1940 - 1960

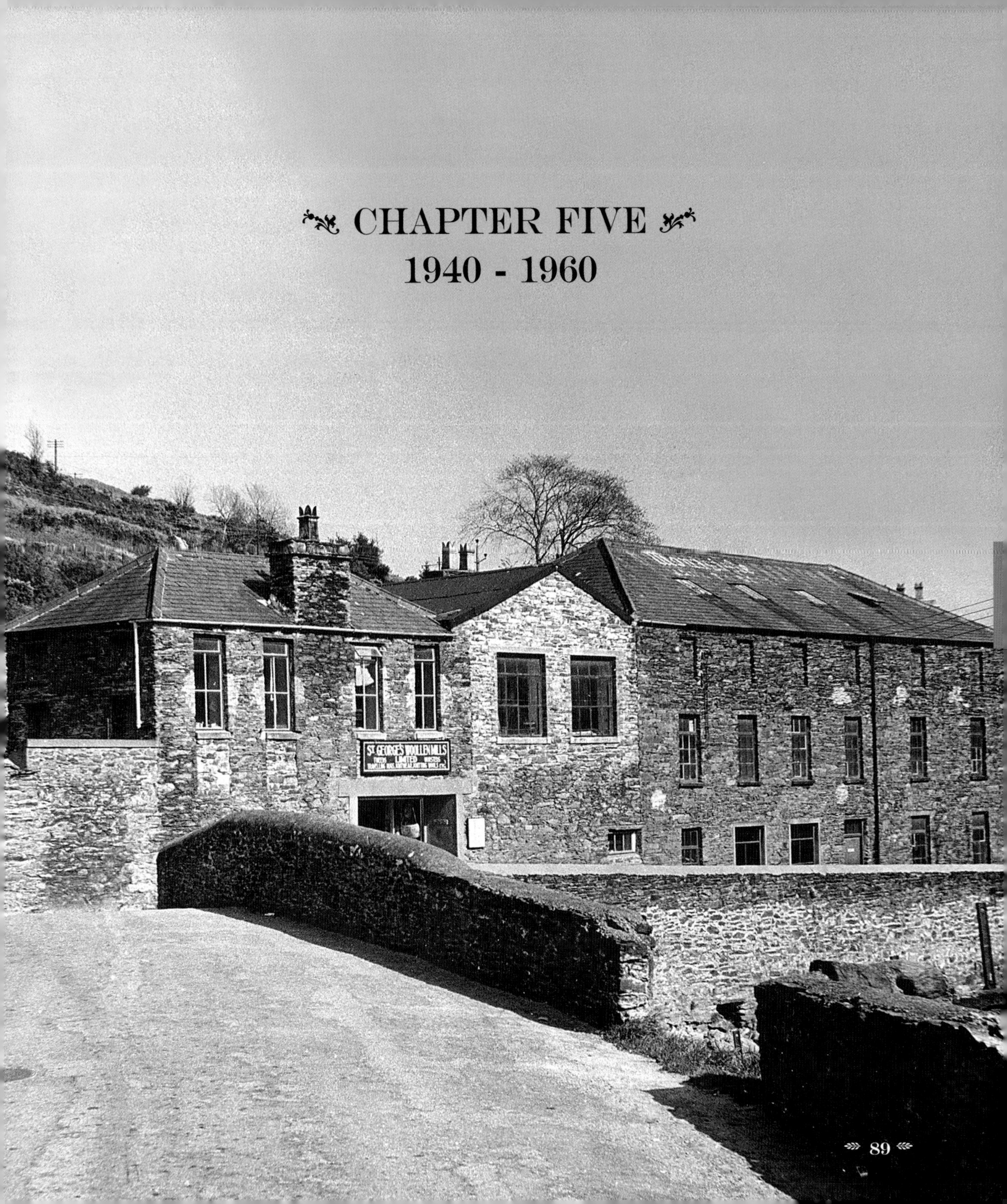
ST. GEORGE'S WOOLLEN MILLS
TWEEDS LIMITED WORSTEDS

Timeline

1940	The evacuation of troops from Dunkirk. Eight Manx steamers were involved in the operation, bringing over 24,000 troops back to England
1942	House of Keys election held at Laxey School
1942-43	Clearance of stone from the Laxey 'Deads' for Island-wide construction work
1943	Laxey acquires its first Fire Station
1944	D-Day. The Allied invasion of Europe
1945	VE Day marking the end of World War Two
1945	Royal visit to Laxey by King George VI and Queen Mary who undertook a 'walkabout' at Laxey MER station
1946	40,000 people visited the Laxey Wheel
1946	Lower Laxey Reading Room re-opened after lying unused during the war
1946	Roof of Laxey Glen Flour Mills destroyed by fire
1947	Extra day's holiday to mark the wedding of Princess Elizabeth
1949	Laxey School purchased their first automatic record player. School meals service started
1949	Houses in Glen Road flooded in October after a deluge of rain
1950	Laxey promenade undermined by a fierce winter storm
1951	Festival of Britain celebrations at Laxey Football Ground
1952	Death of King George VI
1953	Coronation of Queen Elizabeth II. Parties held around the village
1954	Centenary of the Laxey Wheel
1955	Royal visit to the Isle of Man by the Queen and Prince Philip
1956	Laxey Glen Gardens purchased by IOM Forestry Board
1958	Closure and demolition of the Bungalow Hotel halfway up Snaefell mountain
1958	Heavy snow caused major disruption in Laxey

War & Peace

The outbreak of a second world war brought dramatic upheaval to the Isle of Man. Hundreds of servicemen left the home shores to serve King and country, many of them never to return. Manx ships were again requisitioned for the war effort, and unnecessary travel across the Irish Sea quickly became a no-go. The Island's coastline was suddenly on alert for the threat of bombing or invasion, and the usually tranquil Manx countryside was transformed into a base for the training of servicemen and the housing of 'aliens'.

Food, clothing and transport for local residents was limited by allowances and rationing and hotels, guesthouses and even private houses were requisitioned right across the Island, including Laxey, for desperately needed accommodation. And once again war had a disastrous effect on the visiting industry. Visitor numbers, that in 1939 had hovered around the half million mark, plummeted and the Manx Crochet Glove Company was just one example of an enterprise set up to provide employment for 'distressed boarding house keepers'[1].

Fortunately, once hostilities ended, visitors were quick to return for a welcome taste of Manx sun, sand and entertainment. After the war holidaymakers could arrive by aeroplane and from 1946 onwards visitor numbers included air passengers. For a short time the Island enjoyed a boom period with around 600,000 arrivals per year but this soon steadied back to an average half million per year[2].

Out for a walk. Croit-E-Quill near Laxey in 1948

"The end of the war, and the inevitable disillusions of peace, have created an unprecedented urge to get away from home for a complete change... countless thousands are having 'holidays with pay' for the first time in their work-filled lives...1947 sees Manx folk once again offering the traditional Island hospitality to happy holiday makers...The pure air, unpolluted by factory smoke, revives work weary minds and bodies...The Manx climate is equable and sunny, and though humid, distinctly invigorating..."
1947 Isle of Man Official Guide, published by the Isle of Man Publicity Board

In 1949 the Island experienced a serious economic recession. Tourist numbers dropped once again and unemployment rose. But it would take more than this to dampen the Manx spirit for having a good time! By the Fifties Douglas was the Island's recreational capital, with a reputation for top class musical entertainment. Joe Loss and his famous orchestra brought the Big Band sound to the Villa Marina for seasons of nightly dancing, while Jan Ralfini and his orchestra kept thousands of people happy with open air afternoon concerts. Illuminated glens, sports, recreation parks, swimming baths and donkey rides on the beach attracted hordes of eager pleasure seekers. Even eating out was taking on a whole new image. Restaurant dining was no longer the preserve of special occasions and Manx pubs now offered food as well as drink giving rise to the popular new phenomenon of 'pub lunches'.

Make Do and Mend

During the war years it wasn't only food that was subject to rationing. Clothing was also governed by strict allowances and it was seen as not only patriotic but also necessary to 'make do and mend'. From the late Thirties to well after the end of the war the bulk of British wool was all steered towards the manufacture of military uniforms and ordinary families simply had to make the best of what they had. In the Isle of Man wool supplies to housewives were restricted by wool coupons, introduced in 1943.

Uniforms required vast quantities of woollen cloth, particularly woollen serge which was tough, waterproof and hardwearing. This was used for jackets, trousers, overcoats and caps. Flannel was used for underwear and millions of woollen socks were knitted to keep the troops' feet warm and dry. Even away from the field of battle these uniforms were often the best clothing a man owned during the war and many servicemen, and women, remained in uniform for occasions such as dances and weddings.

Wartime became the era of 'utility clothing' where frivolous trimmings were frowned upon and the least quantity of cloth or yarn was used to create wearable outfits. Garments were mended and adapted to get as much wear out of them as possible. Women's everyday woollen clothing

Did you know?

Serge is a sturdy, high quality type of woollen fabric with a distinctive pattern of diagonal ridges. It is flattering to wear as it drapes and hangs well. 'Rough' wool serge is excellent for uniforms and great coats, 'artistic' serge is a finer fabric used for gents and ladies suits.

Old Laxey village c. 1940

THE VILLAGE, OLD LAXEY. I.o.M.   6145

extended to drab shapeless dresses and cardigans, with little in the way of turned up cuffs or over-large lapels, which were viewed as excessive and wasteful. For smart wear the boxy, minimal suit of square-shouldered jacket and short, straight skirt became the norm. Knitting wool was so scarce that recycling of jumpers, socks and cardigans became common practice, with disused items unravelled and made into new garments. Even cat and dog hair was occasionally used as a wool substitute!

Typical British clothing rations. Number of coupons required per item (Total of 66 allocated per year, reduced to 36 per year by 1945):

7 – one woollen dress
14 – one woollen coat
11 – one woollen jacket
5 – one woollen cardigan or jumper
2 – one woollen scarf, pair of gloves or mittens
3 – one yard of woollen cloth, 36" wide
1 – 2 ounces knitting wool

'Utility Clothing During Rationing' Pauline Weston Thomas.

After the war was over it still took a while for clothes rationing to be finally phased out. The British wool industry had to rebuild its export markets, leaving little in the way of new clothing for domestic consumers. In the 1948 Vogue Book of British Exports film stars such as Vivien Leigh and Mai Zettering were used to model outfits made of wool in an attempt to give it a glamorous new image[3].

By the 1940s and '50s the wool market was also being affected by the development of artificial and synthetic fibres. Prior to the Second World War fabrics were mostly of natural origin – silk from the silk worm, wool from the sheep, linen from the flax plant and cotton from the cotton plant. Rayon was already on the market, but in 1939 it was the development of a substance called nylon that really revolutionised clothing. Initially, nylon was used in the manufacture of toothbrushes but was soon discovered to be an excellent replacement for expensive silk in parachutes and ladies stockings. Then came acrylic and polyester, introduced in 1950 and '53 respectively. Acrylic is especially close in texture and appearance to wool and easy to wash. Fortunately for the future of wool though, acrylic doesn't have its thermostatic or waterproof nature, nor does it wear as well and wool remained the fabric of choice for the majority of post-war clothing. Women's fashions relied heavily on wool for skirts, dresses and coats and men once more wore woollen suits for everyday wear.

After the austerity and minimalism of wartime clothing one of the greatest comebacks for women in the Fifties was the triumphant return of the waistline. Fitted underwear gave women shape again and soon the female form was being celebrated in every area of female fashion, from hourglass swimming costumes to full skirts with tiny waists and clinging evening gowns. The ultimate role models for this 'hourglass figure' were screen Goddesses such as Lana Turner and later, Marilyn Monroe. Not that every woman could achieve such perfection. As top British couturier Digby Morton somewhat disparagingly summed up the reasons for the use of muted colours in post-war clothing 'Very few women have good enough figures to emblazon themselves in colour. Expensive clothes are rarely made in bright colours'[4]. Ouch!

Men's suits also witnessed a slight relaxation in the Fifties. Many now featured double-breasted jackets with wide trouser legs and turn-ups, and tweed became super fashionable. Manx tweed was well thought of in this period, described by fashion writers as 'a clever featherweight worsted of crepey effect and crisp handle, yet woven without crepe yarn'[5].

Babies and children were almost uniformly dressed in wool both during and after the war. Garments and accessories for babies and toddlers now included wool frocks, 'buster suits', matinee coats, Spring coats and pram covers.

Knitting also took on a new fashionability in the Fifties. Commercial patterns became widely available and were cleverly marketed, with pictures of handsome 'action' men, wholesome families and attractive young women. Most housewives were expected to be able to knit homemade jumpers and cardigans, and patterns, knitting wool and needles became big sellers.

'Village of the Glens'

In 1940 Laxey apparently offered 'a glamorous pageantry of contrasts', 'a scintillating cocktail of scenery', 'verdant gardens' and a 'sweeping bay with shimmering sea caressing firm silver sands'. Or, at least, it did according to the imaginative writers of the official Laxey Guide books![6] Now dubbed the 'Village of the Glens' its principal attractions in the post-war period were two good fishing rivers; the Glen Gardens with its tea-gardens, dance-floor, boating lake and amusements; and its 'curative' seaweed which, thanks to canny advertising, drew invalids from far and wide – although it's not known whether it actually worked…

Shoppers in Old Laxey, 1948. The Post Office behind the cafe was a hive of activity

Unbeknown to visitors, however, this apparently gentle scenery hid a great deal of sadness. In January 1940 the 'sweeping bay' was the scene of a tragic maritime accident. The Fleetwood trawler 'Merisia' ran aground on rocks at nearby Bulgham Bay during a winter storm and the bodies of her eight crew, including one headless torso, were washed up on Laxey beach.

The impact of war was also keenly felt in the area. A number of children evacuated from England were enrolled in Laxey school and many young men once again left the village to join the armed forces, nineteen of them never to return. In July 1944 the trauma of war came terrifyingly close to home when a Halifax bomber crashed on the southern outskirts of the village during a training flight. Children and parents attending the local school sports day witnessed the stricken plane flying overhead and were distressed by the subsequent explosion in which six RAF servicemen died.

Following the war Laxey settled back into a self-sufficient routine of typical village life. Drawn together by the experiences of war the sense of community was stronger than ever and church groups, clubs and societies abounded. Temperance was still advocated in certain quarters and many Laxey residents, in particular the local branch of the British Women's Total Abstinence Union, tried to encourage 'clean living' among the population. The North Star Lodge of Oddfellows also had a very active 'juvenile' brigade.

Down near the harbour, Lower Laxey was a hub of commercial activity with tea shops, cafes, shops and a post office-cum-shop. Roads were still relatively quiet affording women the luxury of being able to chat in the road while children played nearby. All their daily requirements could be purchased within a small area – from homemade brawn to boots, tins of paint to sweets, fish and chips and freshly baked bread. After work, the men of the family could retire to The Shore hotel where they were guaranteed 'Service with a Smile at Bert's.'

Upper Laxey provided everything the Forties and Fifties housewife could want. Mylroie's drapery was known throughout the Island for linoleum, fur coats, bed linen, clothing and hats. Then there was Corlett the chemist, Johnny Kerruish the Drapers, Miss Cowley the milliner, Skillicorn's for homeware and plumbing, Dibbs the grocer, Granny Gilmore's chips and hot-pot and Annie Kennaugh's fruit and veg shop. Williamson's General Groceries had shops on both sides of New Road as well as a coconut shy and an ice cream kiosk. Number fourteen New Road, one of Egbert Rydings' former houses, was occupied by a barber and in the Co-operative building no less than twenty-seven people were employed, including bakers, cobblers, butchers and coal merchants. Caine's garage ran popular bus tours and Robert Clague came down from Agneash every day to deliver milk around the village in churns. The fishmonger sold his catch around the village with the cry 'Fresh herrin'!'.

A number of manufacturing industries also went quietly about their business in Laxey after the war. Manx Engineering turned out precision instruments at their water-powered factory near the Big Wheel. In Glen Road the St George's Woollen Mill produced quantities of tweed cloth and a number of locals found work at a new carpet factory housed in the old power station. Down by the harbour Erskine's Clothing made men's suits up to and after the war, and produced parachutes during the actual war years. At one time it was so busy that young female workers were bussed in from outlying areas to work there. In 1949 Corlett's Flour Mill stopped work for a major refit but was soon back in full production.

Well-wrapped up visitors on the summit of Snaefell, c. 1950

Laxey was not immune, however, to the serious unemployment that affected the Island in the mid-Fifties. Many families left the village to find work overseas and in 1957 the Government implemented a three year winter work scheme in which local men were employed to clear the remains of the Laxey 'Deads'.

For visitors, little of this hardship was visible. Laxey was promoted as the 'ideal place for a carefree holiday'[7] and droves of tourists still enjoyed electric tram rides or made their way up to Snaefell and the Laxey Wheel. The Glen Gardens, now in public ownership, were the usual hive of activity – with summer carnivals, packed dance floors, wrestling matches and daily entertainment programmes. The village commissioners had provided public tennis courts and bowling greens, and accommodation could be had at any one of fifteen boarding houses and hotels dotted around the valley. The now 'magnificent beach' (according to the guides!) had been prettied up with a retaining wall and walkway. In the summer the promenade thronged with queues of customers hoping for a famous lobster salad at the Wavecrest cafe or warm batch of homemade scones from the End Café.

From 1954 to '59 the official Laxey Guide was simply happy to portray the village as a beautiful little seaport, full of 'olde worlde charm' with an 'almost Continental atmosphere'. Home life was also improving. All houses in the district now had 'the latest sanitary and sewerage arrangements'…

The 'Big Fella'

In the early years of the 1940s the St George's Woollen Mill underwent a major upheaval. After running the business for forty years, Freddie Holroyd finally gave up his day-to-day control of the mill and in 1942 signed over a ten year lease to another Yorkshireman, James Arnold Crawshaw, known as Jim, and London textile merchant Harry Coppel. Crawshaw was to be the face of the business and Coppel a silent business partner.

Crawshaw was just twenty-five when he took charge of the mill but big in both stature and ambitions, and he made an instant impression on Laxey folk. Although his background was fairly humble, having grown up as the son of a Dewsbury blanket manufacturer, locals recall him as a flamboyant character who enjoyed the good life - and ruffled a few feathers along the way. 'Wheeler dealer', 'domineering', 'a big fella and even bigger spender' are just some of the phrases used to describe him.

Initially, Crawshaw and his young wife Mary stayed with Freddie Holroyd at 'Bramble Brae' but they later purchased a grand detached house on the Ramsey Road called 'Isipingo' (after a South African mine), now known as the

'Sycamores'. The house was previously occupied by Francis Reddicliffe, the controversial Mines Captain. Mary, a sweet, educated woman, was reported to be wealthy in her own right and local talk had it that her husband was actually a bankrupt and it was her money that funded the mill and their extravagant lifestyle. They had one daughter, Emma, but the marriage was said to be stormy from the start. Jim made no secret of his love of money and was often seen driving around the village in a big pearl-coloured Daimler with a large cigar in his mouth. Snooker, nightlife and gambling were all favourite pastimes. While living at the Sycamores the Crawshaws employed a local couple as butler and housekeeper but relations were strained and they left after five or six months.

A 1943 Tatham Carding machine

The Laxey mills produced 'Homespun' tweed in great quantities during the war

When Jim Crawshaw took over the St George's Mill the War was at its height and woollen cloth was in big demand. He must have seen this as the perfect opportunity to increase business as, shortly after taking on the lease, he had the Mill completely modernised[8]. Firstly he replaced the old flooring, destabilised through years of vibration and heavy machines, and then installed thousands of pounds worth of new machinery for carding, spinning and weaving which was done on both power looms and Hattersley Domestic foot-operated hand looms. He then set up new companies, based in the mill, for the manufacturing and export of tweed. During the war the Government insisted that all wool produced on the Island be allocated fairly amongst all Manx woollen mills and this was organised by the Wool Control. All raw wool was delivered to the Drill Hall in Douglas from where it was supplied to local manufacturers and any surplus shipped overseas. But by 1943 Crawshaw was already complaining that his supplies were inadequate and he urged the Government to increase his quota[9]. To press his case he even stated that the mill was then employing 60 people but this was probably a rather convenient exaggeration!

Dyeing was no longer carried out by the mill so the old dye house was demolished and a new two-storey section built connecting the drying sheds to the main manufactory. The old willeying sheds were converted into offices and a reception area for Crawshaw, and the now defunct mill race was removed.

For the next few years the push towards exports appears to have been fairly successful. The mill was even listed as a Manx manufacturer in the Vogue Book of British Exports [10] and in 1947 Crawshaw advertised for a new Manager. In the spring of 1948 he took on a new loom tuner, Peter Layton, to look after all the processing.

The advertisement for a new Manager was spotted by an ambitious young Scotsman called Robert Wood. Wood had trained as a weaver and designer at the prestigious Scottish Woollen Technical College and various mills around the Scottish Borders and was keen to advance himself. Unable to find the right opportunity in the Borders he boarded a single propeller canvas plane and flew to the Isle of Man for an interview.

A Handsome Young Scot

Robert Wood, better known as Bob or Jock, was just twenty-three when he first came to the Isle of Man. Darkly handsome and full of energy, he and Crawshaw took a liking to each other. Born in Edinburgh and raised in Galashiels, Bob had hoped to join the RAF when he left school but failed the medical because he couldn't blow the mercury high enough up the tube and wouldn't have been able to handle cabin pressure. He then found work in a factory making blackout blinds and the necessary nature of the work meant he was unable to join any other military services. The area where he lived though was famous for its woollen spinning, weaving and finishing industries so he was soon able to find more stimulating work at the nearby Comelybank Mill. It proved to be a good move. Here he discovered what he really wanted to do with his life. Right from the outset he showed enormous dedication to his new career, working ten hour days in the mill, in all departments, and going to night school four evenings a week. In 1941 he won a bursary to begin training in Wool Manufacture at the world famous Scottish College of Textiles, now called Heriot-Watt College. With typical single-mindedness he immersed himself in his studies, completing his final exams

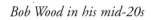

Bob Wood in his mid-20s

Comelybank Woollen Mill, Galashiels, since demolished

four years later with a raft of first class passes and a Bronze intermediate examination medal.

The Bronze medal awarded to Bob Wood by the Scottish College of Textiles

Bob obviously made an impression on Jim Crawshaw, who quickly offered him the job of Mill Manager. Soon he was lodging happily at the Ravenscliffe Guest House on the New Road and on the 1st of July 1948 he took up his new post. Not that he had long to settle in. Shortly afterwards Crawshaw took Bob on a colourful road trip around Europe, driving as far as Yugoslavia which had been destroyed after the war. Along the way the two young men did lots of buying and selling – mixed with a fair amount of pleasure. Their journey only came to an end after Crawshaw hit the gaming tables in Monte Carlo and gambled away large amounts of money.

Once back in Laxey Bob quickly took over the running of the mill, keeping a close eye on costings, wages and prices. But Crawshaw's ambitious plans had overstretched him and in June 1949 Bob watched his dreams evaporate as the company went into voluntary liquidation. The process took two long drawn out years to complete, many staff left, including loom tuner Peter Layton, and a lot of the plant and equipment had to be sold off, including the spinning and finishing plants. Humiliated and considerably poorer, Jim Crawshaw turned his back on the Isle of Man and left to try his fortune in South Africa. Little was heard of him for some years until an item in the local press reported that he had been killed in a car crash. It was a sad, ignominious end for a man who had made his reputation with high living and expensive tastes.

Bob Wood, meanwhile, was still determined to pursue his career in woollen manufacture even though the odds seemed stacked against him. His main talents lay in design and practical weaving but at the age of just twenty-five he had been left with a stripped-out factory in an already depressed economy. Then a near miracle happened. In February 1950 Freddie Holroyd put the St George's Mill up for sale and Bob and a group of hastily gathered shareholders were able to buy the business from the liquidators. Fortunately in his first years in the Isle of Man he had made a close circle of friends and associates including Harry Halsall, Tom Mylchreest and Eric Teare and managed to persuade them to help in the venture.

Just under one year later, on January 22nd 1951, the new St George's Woollen Mills company held their Annual General Meeting. Bob Wood was now a shareholder and Managing Director, and alongside him sat two experienced woollen manufacturers, Haviland Mann from Bradford and Ralph Howarth from the Sulby woollen mills. This first meeting, however, must have been tinged with anxiety. Wool prices were heading for a post-war peak and supplies of yarn from woollen spinners in Yorkshire and Scotland were hard to come by. It was not going to be an easy ride.

1951 signalled the start of a new chapter in the mill's history – but it also ended on a reflective note. In October that year Freddie Holroyd died at his Douglas home, aged 74, after a day out motoring with his wife. Although he had long retired from the mill, he had still maintained his interest in the woollen business right throughout his life, latterly working as a Wool Controller for the Manx Government.

New Life in An Old Mill

Bob Wood wasted no time in breathing new life into the Laxey mill. At least six double width power looms had been left behind in the changeover but there was no-one to set them up properly so he contacted Peter Layton, who had gone to work in Yorkshire as a power loom tuner, and Eric Howarth, the son of Mill director Ralph Howarth, also a trained tuner and weaver. Both agreed to come and work for Bob and they soon had everything up and running and started training new weavers to operate the looms. Only one Hattersley Domestic Pedal Loom remained but that was single width and used occasionally for demonstrations and small runs of cloth.

Eric Howarth was also appointed as the mill's Sales Manager and he quickly organised reliable sales reps around the country and linked up with export agencies in Canada and Belgium. Bob himself made a number of selling trips to London.

St George's mill now had two central strands to its business. The Laxey Woollen Company Ltd handled manufacturing and exports, and The Island Woollen Company Ltd was established to promote the mill's products locally. Although passionate about the success of the mill, Bob was still very much accountable to the other shareholders

Eric Howarth,
Mill sales manager

who were mostly accountants, and these were tricky times. Sources of ready-spun yarn were just one of the headaches and he often had to buy in cheap job-lots. This meant colour continuity wasn't exactly reliable and some of the least popular colours, such as bright yellow and orange, remained up in the top floor for long years afterwards! It also meant that many items were 'one-offs' as further supplies of certain colours couldn't be assured.

Nevertheless, the mill was still able to produce a good range of tartans, worsted dress cloth, travelling rugs, worsted 'bird's-eye' suitings and hand-knitted items. One of the mill's biggest customers in these early days was 'Messrs Fashionwear' of London. On occasion they would even send their dress designer Mrs Sinclair to Laxey to discuss orders and requirements. The cloth was all produced in-house but the hand knitting was done by several local outworkers and exclusive hand knitted items proved to be good money makers.

New retail arrangements were vital to the success of the 'new' mill and an important step forwards came with the setting up of a small shop on the ground floor of what was formerly the old 'drying shed'. A side door and large window were installed facing out onto the Glen Road so that, for the first time, locals and passing tourists could actually see what the mill produced and call in to buy knitting wool, patterns, needles, jumpers, gloves and cloth. To catch extra visitors

A busy day at a 1950s Manx agricultural show

on their way to the beach a small wooden hut opened for business down near the harbour but this was shortlived and the outlet was soon transferred up to the Rose Gardens at the western end of the tram station. Cloth from the mill was also displayed at Fletcher's Douglas showroom and supplied to several leading tailors. As early as the summer of 1950 Bob was ready to promote the mill's new name and image to the wider community and in August he and his staff set up a stand at the Southern Agricultural show.

Early the following year it was decided the mill needed a thorough re-organisation and work was stopped for two months. All the old shafting used to provide power from the water wheel was removed, an upstairs room in the old drying sheds was turned into Wood's design office (albeit with a ceiling made of old packing cases!), the mending department was established next door and adjacent to that the all-important tool room where the loom tuners made and fixed machinery. All weaving was done on the middle floor and yarn and warp preparation was carried out in the top floor. A new hoist was fixed to the outside of the top floor door so that yarn could be lifted upstairs without going through the building.

By the end of the season the mill was back in full swing, producing a range of hundreds of patterns in many different weight cloths. The mill now had 40 accounts with customers in Scotland and England and an additional shop in busy Castle Street in Douglas.

> 'Each loom is now driven by individual electric motors and there is no shafting whatsoever. The machinery is of the latest design and productivity is high.' (Impressions of the Laxey Mill, Barbara Anderson 1954)

As wool prices were rising again Bob tried to obtain Manx wool but this was conditional on being able to spin it. His only option was to install a completely new yarn manufacturing plant on the ground floor and a new willeying machine was installed in one of the outhouses. It was also agreed that a new dyeing facility should be set up and by the end of the year the mill once again had carding, spinning and dyeing machinery in place.

Bob was trading in difficult times though, and in 1953 poor sales led to a build-up of excess stock. Fortunately the mill had good custom from the Manx Museum which sent the fleece from its small flock of Loaghtan sheep to the mill for processing into knitting wool. The wool went through eight separate processes – scouring, willeying, carding, spinning, doubling, scouring, hanking and bundling before it was ready for sale.

The following year the Mill was forced to operate on a three-day working week

20th March 1951 Ordered by the Erskine Clothing Manufacturing Company – 'Ruskin Worsted', value of £62, length 35.5, price per yard 35/4. Delivered to the Quay, Laxey.
(1947-57 mill order book)

Section of a 1943 Tatham Carding machine

1952 Stock list - Worsted cloths, woollen cloths, travel rugs, knee rugs, cot blankets, pram rugs, white blankets, scarves, knitting wools, knitwear, gloves, sheepskins, needles, crochet hooks.

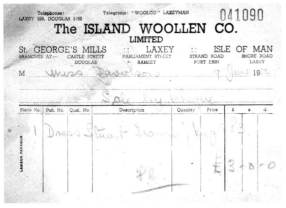

The Island Woollen Co. was the 1950s operating name of the Laxey Woollen Mills

from January to June and for the next three months production was closed down entirely. America was one of the mill's main targets in the Fifties and it was hoped that they would be tempted by the original qualities of Manx wool. Hundreds of sample books were sent across the Atlantic but, disappointingly, they were all rejected as tailors wouldn't work with it and the mill once again had to revert to buying in yarn.

Closer to home Bob concentrated on expanding the mill's local retail outlets. Wholesaling had slumped and at one stage he even noted, somewhat prophetically, that *'if this state of affairs continues it would appear that before long the clothing industry will be governed by a very few, big multiple people'* [11].

May Brew operating a power loom

Having been rebuffed by the United States Bob tried another tack and looked to European exports as a way forward. Initially, the company approached Denmark, Holland, Belgium, Switzerland and Sweden and this time his tactics paid off. The orders started coming in. By mid-1955 the mill was using nine power looms and high quality 'Ruskin worsteds' and tweed were being shipped to numerous countries. Within a year they had extended their markets to include Italy, Japan, Canada, New Zealand and Australia. Eventually, with the lure of finer, lightweight fabrics, even America was persuaded to join the party.

In 1956 my parents bought me a Laxey-made travel rug to take to prep school. My Dad was in charge of the Royal Air Force base at Jurby so I chose the rug for its predominantly blue colour. Since my school days the same rug has travelled with me to the Malayan jungle, Oman, Cyprus and all around Europe and now enjoys a quiet life on the sofa of my Douglas apartment...
(Bill Chacksfield, Chief Executive of the Isle of Man Post Office)

The Birth of Manx Tartan

Up until the mid-Fifties the Laxey mill produced cloth woven from tartan designs originating largely from Scotland. The use of tartan in Scotland goes back hundreds of years to the days when clan chiefs wore it to indicate their rank. In those days, however, they relied on natural dyes which varied from one area to another and most clans soon developed a distinctive shade or pattern of cloth particular to their district. Tartan, therefore soon became a symbol of clan identity.

Then came the devastating Battle of Culloden in 1745 and tartan was banned for the following thirty-six years, in which time many original designs disappeared. Within a century though, it was back in popularity and by the twentieth century there were so many tartans coming on the market that modern designs had to be officially registered[12]. Many 'false' tartans also sprang up – these are fabrics woven to look like tartan but lacking in taste, history and correct patterning. Such tartans are known as bumbee tartans and these are not officially recognised.

True tartans are basically divided into five types of design[13]. Modern features strong, vivid colours made possible by today's chemical dyes. Hunting is a practical, darker type of tartan developed as hillside camouflage by the gentry of the Highland estates. Dress tartan is made up of brighter colours and used for formal and high-ranking military occasions. Ancient is based on twenty-one colours which duplicate the shades produced by early natural dyes. Weathered (also known as 'muted' or 'reproduction') imitates the appearance of tartan cloth made from vegetable dyes and worn many years in Highland weather.

Tartan was widely worn by the Manx in the nineteenth century, but not necessarily for reasons of style. Lord Teignmouth, writing in 1829, noted that

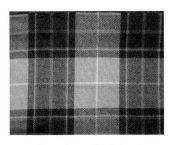

A section of original Manx tartan

'Manks women…are also particularly fond of showy colours and wear much the tartan; this propensity is occasionally severely rebuked from the pulpit. The cheapness and variety of the tartan form its chief recommendation to the Manks' [14].

Initially, tartan was used to represent individual families or clans but when Norway decided to adopt its own national tartan this sowed the seed for other countries to follow. In 1957 a Manx cultural organisation called Ellynyn ny Gael, or 'Arts of the Gael', suggested that the Isle of Man should adopt a national tartan. Local designers were invited to send in their ideas and Patricia 'Paddy' McQuaid of Ramsey was selected for her winning pattern based on the colours of the Island's landscape – green, purple, white, yellow, blue, dark blue and rowan red [15]. The Manx tartan was registered on November 3rd 1959 [16] and in 1961 the Laxey Woollen Mills began producing it for Miss McQuaid to sell through her shop in Ramsey and the mill company sold it under licence to the rest of the world. But the agreement only lasted a couple of years, upon which production of the Manx tartan transferred to Moore's Mill at St Johns.

Power to the Loom

Tourist guides from the 1950s referred to the mill as one of a number of 'charming rural industries' in Laxey - but this was probably being a little generous! By the mid-Fifties the Mill was actually a highly mechanised manufacturing centre dominated by huge black Hodgson power looms which each produced tremendous clattering noise and vibration. On the ground floor there were two large carding machines which ran the full length of the building and took up the left side of the room. On the right hand side was a large, clanking spinning mule which also ran the full length of the building. In fact the machinery took up so much space that the weavers had to enter the weaving room via a tiny doorway on the first floor.

Bill Gill operating the warp mill in the Laxey mills

The spun yarn was sent up to the top floor by block and tackle and placed on the warp, a big wheel-like machine about seven feet wide and six feet in diameter onto which the coloured yarns were wound in their set order. From here the yarn was transferred onto a weaver's beam (like a long giant wooden bobbin) which was lowered down through the trapdoor and placed on the looms on the middle floor. One worker would usually operate two looms at a time and the power looms made such a noise that workers had to communicate by lip reading. Permanent hearing damage among power loom weavers was a common problem.

The main difference between pre and post-war weaving was the sex of the loom operators. Traditionally weaving had always been the preserve of men, but women had dominated factory work during the war and female weavers now almost outnumbered men. After the war skilled weavers were hard to come by so it simply made sense to train whoever was willing to learn.

Female power loom operatives in the Laxey Woollen Mills

Once the cloth was woven it was carefully taken off the loom and transferred to the mending room where it underwent rigorous checking by three or four girls. This was a highly skilled job that had changed little since the nineteenth century. Even the tiniest hole or knot could mean the cloth being rejected by potential buyers and the mending room foreman required strict discipline and total concentration from his workers. When the webs of cloth were deemed perfect, tweeds and rugs were sent to the St John's mill to be finished and finer worsted fabrics were sent to England or Scotland.

Linda Brew operating a Hodgson power loom. The noise was deafening

Cloth mending at St George's Woollen mills

In 1950 the staffing of the mill was something of a close-knit affair. That year a group of local teenage girls turned up at the mill looking for work and ended up being hired as a 'job lot'. Two of them were sisters, Linda and May Brew. Linda had only gone along for a laugh but ended up being hired anyway! Within days the girls were being trained up and were soon put to work on the power looms.

Peter and Linda Layton (nee Brew), former employees of the Laxey Woollen Mills

'In the early Fifties the mill had a cat (a useful member of staff, as mice could do major damage to cloth!). At the weekends I would put the cat in a cardboard box, place it on the front of my motorbike and take it back to my lodgings for the weekend. On Monday I would bring it back the same way'
(Mill employee Peter Layton 1950-55)

For May this was the beginning of a lifetime career and she worked as a weaver in the mill for most of her working life. Linda married the weaving foreman Peter Layton and the couple left Laxey to live in Northern Ireland where they both continued to work in the woollen industry.

Workers at the mill nearly all lived in Laxey during this period but not all were Manx and those that weren't tended to live in lodgings. Most workers would either walk or cycle to work or occasionally come by motorcycle.

By the late Fifties the mill had settled into a fairly stable organisation. There were about twelve employees working at the mill at that time. Aside from myself, apprenticed to the engineer, there was Don Cain from Douglas, Ian Mackie, Harry Leech from Halifax and Jimmy Kinrade – originally a Laxey miner. Jimmy was a useful fella who made up the bales and did lots of other jobs. Bill Gill, a former lithographer from Croit-e-Quill, worked the warp mill. The weavers were nearly all women – two Manx girls May Brew and Shirley Kermode, and Doris Sykes, Maud Nutter and Nellie Hellawell from Lancashire. Stanley Cockburn was the foreman and a loom tuner. Stan was a bit of an entertainer out of hours – a good singer who took part in concerts and helped out at the Methodist Youth Club.
(Mill employee Peter Creer 1955-63)

Shop, Shop, Shopping

The retail side of the St George's Woollen Mill only became properly organised in the early 1950s and the company was able to ride a wave of new enthusiasm for shopping. Outfitters had a tendency to call themselves 'Messrs' and offered addresses including cable and telegram codes. Orders were handwritten or typed on wafer thin buff-coloured paper and the difference between the flamboyant typefaces used by American companies and the 'proper' style of London couturiers neatly sums up the mood of the times.

In the Isle of Man, the mill aimed to capture the visitor market and outlets were quickly established in Laxey's electric railway station and other busy tourist hotspots. Castle Street in Douglas was a perfect choice as it was a thriving shopping street in the late Fifties, backing onto a promenade lined with guest houses. The mill shop here was run for many years by Bob Wood's mother-in-law, known always to her customers as Mrs Hulley. Within a few years outlets were also opened in Ramsey's main street and Port Erin's Strand Road leading down to the beach. Both towns had white sandy beaches, parks and packed summer seasons and drew thousands of visitors every year. At the mill shops tourists could buy their travel rugs, gloves and scarves, and locals had everything the home knitter could need.

But the mill didn't just sell from conventional retail outlets. Large, high-end hotels such as the Fort Anne attracted plenty of wealthy visitors and the mill installed stylish display cabinets in their foyers so that guests could purchase Manx goods without having to leave the premises.

To promote the St George's name to the public, the mill also took regular stands at the Island's annual agricultural shows where weaving foreman Peter Layton would set up a hand loom and demonstrate the traditional art of weaving.

From 1954 to 59 the Mill adverts recommended customers look for 'the Ruskin mark on the cloth' but by 1960 this was changed to 'look for the Manxmark on the cloth.' The Manxmark was a symbol of quality introduced by Tynwald in the late 1950s to promote locally produced goods and protect against imitation[17]. Manufacturers had to be granted permission to use it and the St George's Mill was granted its ManxMark certification in 1957. Strict conditions had to be satisfied as to 'quality, purity, cleanliness and method of production'[18] and approved Manxmark products included kippers, honey, beer, wools, tweeds, carpets and some agricultural produce. The life of the Manxmark was, however, only brief. The mill printed it on their labels up until the mid-Sixties but, as an entity, it never achieved the high profile that was intended for it and quietly went out of use.

Advertisement for the popular Fort Anne Hotel, Douglas 1958

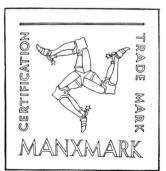

The Laxey Woollen Mill's Manxmark certificate

Young Sally Wood

Highs and Lows

By the mid-Fifties Bob Wood had established a challenging role for himself in the commercial life of the Isle of Man. But his days weren't all work and no play. At the time of his arrival in the village the male population was on the decline and the appearance of a good-looking, unattached man who owned his own car and had good prospects caused quite a stir! The lively entertainment scene in Fifties Douglas also suited Bob well. During his college years in Scotland he had partly funded his studies by singing and playing the piano with Joe McBurney's Dance Band and when he moved to the Isle of Man he became a regular at Saturday afternoon tea dances and spent many a night listening to the Joe Loss orchestra. After a number of years enjoying the life of a carefree bachelor he fell for a pretty young girl called Sally Hulley, who sometimes helped her mother out at the Mill shop.

On the 14th February 1957 Bob and Sally were married. She was 18, he was 32 and despite the age gap it proved to be an enduring marriage. In 1958 they had their first child, a daughter Dian, and the following year a son, John, was born.

At the time of their marriage the fortunes of the Laxey Woollen Mills appeared to be on the up. Bob was employing at least ten workers[19], the local shops were doing well, the mill's reputation was growing again and orders were now flooding in from the U.S. Many British orders were even turned down as a result. But then, suddenly, disaster struck.

In 1957 American authorities introduced a tariff on the import of British woollens, forcing up the price of Laxey's products to untenable levels. Bob Wood faced a huge dilemma. Most of the season's stock had already been made but they could no longer sell it to the American market and it was too late to secure any more British orders. Although the mill was now using nine power looms it couldn't compete with much bigger mills in Scotland and Yorkshire and Bob had no choice but to bring production to a halt. Thankfully, the success of the mill's retail arm ensured its survival through the remaining years of the Fifties but if it was to keep going much longer a whole new approach was needed. The mill was about to change direction once again.

References:

1. Minutes of Meeting of War Committee of Tynwald 26th August 1943, IOM Public Record Office
2. IOM Examiner annuals, MNH
3. 'Vogue Book of British Exports' No.1, Vol.6 Special Supplement on Wool publ. Conde Nast Publications, London 1948
4. ibid.
5. ibid.
6. Laxey Official guides 1939-1950
7. Laxey official guide 1955 MS F78 MNH
8. Barbara Anderson Unpublished thesis, Ref.M677.3 Douglas Library
9. Minutes of War Committee of Tynwald July 1st 1943, IOM Public Record Office
10. Vogue Book of British Exports 1949 p.63
11. 1954 Laxey Woollen Mill Manager's Report
12. www.scran.ac.uk (in partnership with the Royal Commission on Ancient and Historical Monuments of Scotland)
13. Borders Textile book
14. 'Sketches of the Coasts and Islands of Scotland, the Isle of Man' V.II Lord Teignmouth, John Parker, London 1836
15. Manninagh No.1 May 1972 p.17
16. IOM Examiner 17th July 1981, MNH
17. Manx Year Book 1964, Norris Meyer Press, Douglas p.6
18. Manxmark brochure produced by Ray Linton Ltd.
19. 'The Isle of Man - A Study In Economic Geography' J.W.Birch, Cambridge University Press 1964 fig.43 p.167

A D-81 Foot Treadle Loom
made by
George Hattersley & Sons

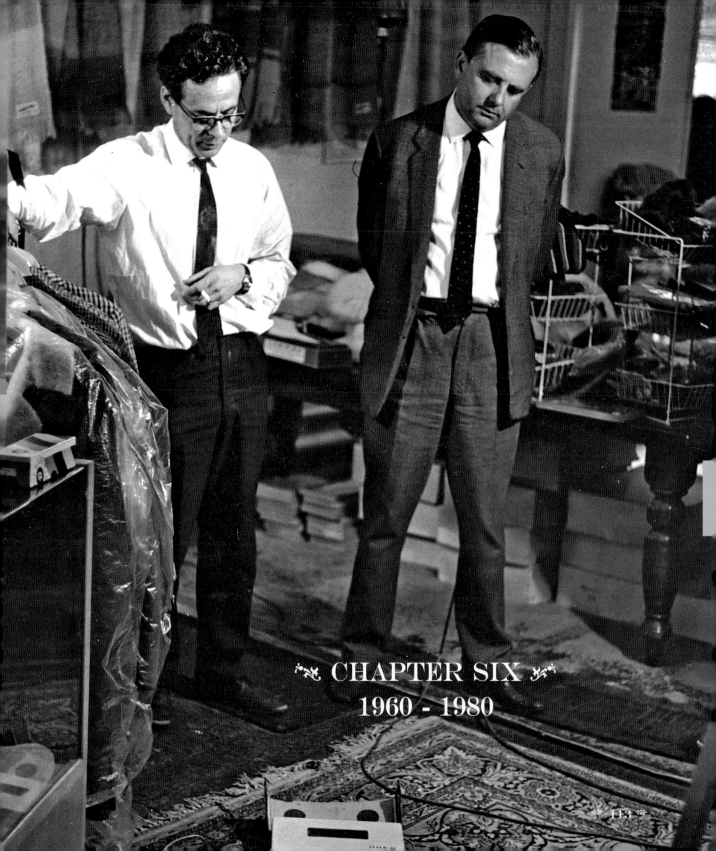

CHAPTER SIX
1960 - 1980

Timeline

1960 Inaugural modern Parish Walk, an 85-mile challenge

1962 IoM Steam Packet launch their first car ferry – 'The Manx Maid'

1963 Heavy snow in February closes Laxey school

1963 Visit to Laxey's Valley Gardens by the Queen Mother

1966 National Seamen's strike causes major disruption to the tourist season

1965 The Manx Government buys the Laxey Wheel and begins a restoration programme

1969 'Turning' ceremony for the restored Laxey Wheel, attended by 10,000 people

1971 Revival of Laxey's traditional Victorian Village Fair

1971 Ownership of Laxey's Valley Gardens transferred to the Village Commissioners

1973 Summerland fire disaster. More than 50 people died and over 80 were seriously injured

1973 Laxey Harbour closed to commercial traffic

1977 Queen's Silver Jubilee parties held all over Laxey

1979 Millennium of Tynwald, celebrating one thousand years of continuous government in the Isle of Man

1979 Laxey School Golden Jubilee

1979 A busy year for VIP visitors to Laxey. Firstly, Princess Anne, followed by the Lord Mayor of London and then the President of Malta…

1979 BBC 'Blue Peter' presenter John Noakes opens the Cavalcade of Trams in Laxey

Sunbeds and Sangria

In the 1960s and '70s the Island played host to a succession of important visitors. Firstly, Queen Elizabeth II and the Queen Mother paid a royal visit. The following year it was the turn of Princess Margaret and Lord Snowdon. Then in 1970 the Duke of Edinburgh visited and two years later he was back again, but this time with the Queen. Oh, and in 1964 a rebellious new rock band called the Rolling Stones played a concert on the Isle of Man, but the older generation didn't know quite what to make of them...

Unfortunately ordinary visitors were choosing to head **away** from the Isle of Man as the introduction of package holidays saw holidaymakers fly off to warm, sunny European destinations. Spain became an instant hit and the Island struggled to compete. By 1966 Ramsey, with its swaying palm trees, was being advertised as the 'Manx Costa Brava' to try and persuade holidaymakers into rethinking their travel plans!

In the Seventies the Island was keen to promote its comprehensive travel links with the rest of Britain. Ronaldsway airport was 'linked to cities all over the UK' and the Isle of Man Steam Packet proudly advertised its 'three modern car ferries with drive-on, drive-off facilities' ferrying passengers to and from Liverpool, Ardrossan, Fleetwood, Llandudno, Heysham, Belfast and Dublin.

Those visitors who were lured into spending their precious holidays on Manx soil were greeted by a scene of vibrant new glamour, displayed mainly at the Casino, the Villa Marina, the Cabaret at the Palace and funky discotheques around the Island. Douglas promenade was lit with dazzling illuminations; Ken Dodd, Jimmy Tarbuck and Max Bygraves kept the laughs coming; the Tremeloes, Marmalade and Roger Whittaker entertained with music, song and a bit of whistling. And to everyone's delight, in the late 1970s the Island was bathed in hot sunshine...

But even on days when the sun wasn't shining the Isle of Man had an extra card up its sleeve. Summerland and the Aquadrome were built in 1971 to great fanfare – advertised as 'the largest indoor resort in the world'. This state-of-the-art, climate controlled entertainment complex featured expansive deck-chair terraces, garden restaurants and bars, a funfair, amusement arcade, discos and the giant Sundome 'for a quick suntan under infra-red and ultra-violet rays'.

Tragically, the Summerland dream came to a devastating end in 1973 when the building was destroyed by a blaze that took the lives of more than fifty people.

"A Charming, Old-World Village..."

In 1960 Laxey had a population of just over one thousand. The village was close-knit and lively with flourishing shops and a feeling of general prosperity. All the traders knew each other and helped each other out and the Village Commissioners certainly felt it was the perfect destination for 'the ideal and carefree holiday...'

'Laxey is a charming old-world village...with a peaceful bay and tiny harbour. Tall cliffs shelter the popular beach and promenade. In the village are the Glen Gardens and the start of the Snaefell Mountain Railway line which climbs to the summit of the Island's highest point through impressive, unspoilt scenery. Laxey is the home of the world's largest waterwheel, now 119 years old and preserved as an engineering masterpiece. Sailing enthusiasts will find a delightful little tidal port. There is a camping site in the valley and a youth hostel overlooks the village.' (1960's Official Guide to Laxey published by the Village Commissioners)

Unfortunately the official Isle of Man brochure for 1962 hinted that this wasn't the complete picture - 'the river offers no attractions to the angler', 'the beach, ...stony close up to the promenade', 'the Laxey Glen Gardens...have fallen into disrepair but efforts are being made to rehabilitate them and restore them to their former beauty'[1]. Oh dear.

Not that this deterred summer visitors from descending on Laxey in their thousands. Many people arrived by tram and could then enjoy a walk to the beach or Wheel or hop onto the locally-run minibus which ran between the two. If you had a sense of adventure you could stay up the hill at the Axnfel Youth Hostel but if you fancied something a bit more comfortable there was always the Ravenscliffe Private Hotel with its 'Spring interior beds...'

And visitors could always go home with any number of locally made souvenirs which were available throughout the village. The Meerschaum pipe factory had set up a flourishing business in the old warehouse down by the harbour and St George's Woollen Mills ties, scarves and travel rugs were on sale at its own retail outlets and the White House café. It wasn't all hard-nosed commercialism either – 'until recently the last foreman of the mines sat at his gate to sell posies of flowers to the passing visitors'[2].

Laxey was also an enjoyable and busy place to live in the Sixties. The White House Café on New Road was a popular destination for smart lunches and tea outings, the End Café on the Promenade served 'Pots of tea on the beach' and the Wave Crest Café offered a 'Continental-style tea garden and kiosk where fresh coffee, minerals, teas, ices and postcards may be obtained.' For a real Manx taste of the Sixties, delicious Felice's ice cream and Quirk's bread and cakes could be bought at the Fairy Cottage Stores at the top of Old Laxey Hill. Nightlife was based on a chat and a pint at one of the many local pubs, unless you were feeling energetic in which case you could dance the night away at 'Ye Olde Coach and Horses' which boasted 'the only licensed discotheque on the Island with live D.J'. Outdoor sport was well provided for with facilities for tennis, bowling, putting, and football at the sports grounds on Glen Road.

The mill shop in the Sixties, now a wood working studio

The New Road was still the lively commercial area of the village. Mr Kinrade had his wholesale tobacconist shop, then there was Cowley the painter and decorator, the Co-op for all household needs opposite the Commissioner's office and wonderful smells from Kinrade's Bakery run by Jack Kaighen.

Since the demise of the mining industry the land in the base of the valley alongside the Woollen Mills had looked sad and neglected, dominated by huge piles of waste stone known as the 'deads'. But as these were gradually removed a suitable space was created for the construction of the Cooil Roi elderly person's housing complex which was completed in 1967. In the Seventies the adjoining Valley Gardens were developed into a public parkland with an extensive programme of planting and landscaping.

In 1971 the Laxey Fair or 'Feailley Laxa' was revived on that very spot. With the growth of the mining industry and population in the mid nineteenth century the

Fair had moved from the river mouth to the Washing Floors and was held on Good Friday. As mining had dwindled the traditional Fair also lapsed, but when celebrations were held to mark the restoration of the Laxey Wheel it was seen as a good opportunity to reinstate the Fair. August was chosen as the new date, participants were encouraged to dress in Victorian clothing and, although there was no longer any cattle trading, there was still plenty of singing, dancing and merry-making.

By the Seventies Laxey was being promoted as a good place for a 'lazey-dazey holiday'. Words like solitude, mental relaxation, old world charm and rest-cum-health resort are sprinkled liberally through the visitor guides of the day. 'The general consensus of opinion is that Laxey is a beauty spot first and always, with a bit of gaiety thrown in'[3].

Sweater Girls to Tank Tops

The Sixties and Seventies were boom years for the fashion industry. This was the era when casual dress became more prominent, women started wearing trousers for reasons other than work and 'anything went'. Hip young designers like Mary Quant and Ralph Lauren began to make their mark, raising hemlines to unprecedented levels and transforming models like Twiggy into

A 1960s advertising photograph for the Laxey Woollen Mills

personalities in their own right. At the start of the Sixties hemlines were still below the knee and the shape was, well, shapeless, but in 1967 a daring, super-short garment known as the miniskirt hit the high streets and suddenly there was no looking back.

Wool enjoyed many guises in the Sixties. Formal wear found stylish new status with the woollen suit developed by Chanel and Dior, bringing a slimline elegance to the female form. American icons still held great sway, in particular Jackie Kennedy whose neat two piece suits with three quarter length sleeves and wide collars were widely imitated. Men still wore suits and ties for everyday wear, usually with hats. Checked designs became popular for both sexes in dog, hound's-tooth or Prince of Wales check. Beneath their jackets, the man's sweater was a wardrobe staple, sometimes featuring diagonal checks and in a wide variety of colours. And men were still men. Knitting pattern books of the time show immaculately attired male models, carrying garden implements or puffing on pipes. By contrast female knitwear models are usually shown paired up with shopping companions, hair beautifully coiffured and 'smart yet casual'.

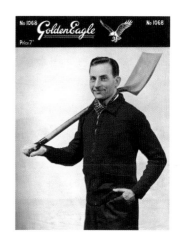

The more casual styles that emerged in the Sixties were led by the younger generation. Energetic new styles of dancing gave rise to the addition of 'kick pleats' in straight woollen skirts and the 'sweater girl' brought a new sexiness to the woolly jumper. Knitted twin sets were still worn but often as separates. Pinafore dresses in plain or check wool fabrics were now teamed with polo neck jumpers or tie neck blouses. Narrow shouldered coat dresses were worn with or without a fitted, skinny rib sweater underneath.

"Before the days of tumble driers many women lay their washed, rung out knitwear in paper tissue and then brown paper. They put it to dry under a carpet for two days. When it was removed from the tissue, the footsteps that had pounded over the knit gave it a flat, dry cleaned, as-new appearance." (Pauline Weston Thomas fashion-era.com)

A wide variety of influences determined the direction of clothing in the Sixties and Seventies. Hip new pop bands such as the Beatles introduced new colour and clothing combinations which were transmitted into people's homes by fashion photography and the advent of television. Rock festivals, pop art and the freedom of the hippy movement were translated into freedom of clothing and the birth of high street chain stores made buying such clothing suddenly easier.

By 1970 hemlines were dictated more by mood than anything. Women had a wide range of styles available to them from the short mini skirt, to the midi skirt, maxi dress, or even hot pants. The Laxey mill cottoned on to this trend by producing women's tartan kilts in both short and long lengths. Woollen, crepe and jersey trousers and trouser suits were both highly acceptable with the width of the trouser hemline flaring out then straightening in again as the decade progressed. In the evening the full length formal dress was overtaken by full length maxi dresses, loose kaftans, evening trousers or glamorous halter neck catsuits.

Ladyship WOOLS

In 5 sizes to fit
24 to 32 inch chest
Ladyship County or
Safari Crepe Double Knitting
PRICE 7½p

Good heating in cars, houses and shops made the long wool coat less of a necessity and the shorter car coat became a firm favourite. For a casual alternative to the bulky jumper the sleeveless tank top was a popular favourite, and by the late Seventies knitwear designers such as Bill Gibb were making complex, brightly coloured hand knits trendy, especially in chunky cardigans. This was something of a boon era for hand knitters as long knitted wool scarves, ponchos, berets and footless leg warmers became the 'in-thing' [4].

Ladyship WOOLS

Poncho: 21 ozs.
Skirt and Bolero: 17 or 19 ozs.
Ladyship County Double Knitting or
Safari Double Crepe
PRICE 5p. (ONE SHILLING)

In the mid Seventies a young pop band from Scotland suddenly made tartan ultra fashionable with young girls. The Bay City Rollers had a short but colourful career and for a brief period their wide, slightly-too-short tartan trousers and scarves spawned a teenage tartan army of adoring fans. The backlash came when the punk movement got hold of tartan and dirty kilts became a symbol of rebellion and anarchy. Luckily, that trend was also shortlived.

A Hand Loom Renaissance

As Sixties' fashions moved into top gear the Wood family, trying to make a go of the Laxey Woollen mills, realised they needed to make some big decisions if they were to keep up and satisfy the Mill's shareholders. Faced by shrinking visitor numbers and fierce competition from larger mills in England and Scotland Bob knew he had to try something radical. His own experience and passion lay in hand loom weaving and with this in mind he decided to take what some people saw as a risky step backwards – getting rid of the power looms and replacing them with traditional hand looms.

A hand loom weaver can only produce one hundred yards of cloth a week but has the advantage of being able to produce short runs of high quality, hand-made products in exclusive designs. Bob's hope was that by creating finer, lighter weight fabrics than previously possible the cloth would have greater appeal to international buyers in the high-end market. In his own words, if the mill was to survive, the only possible way out was to try a little 'snob appeal' [5].

Bob's decision marked the beginning of a decade of major upheaval. In early 1963 four of the mill's power looms were dispensed with and replaced by two all-wooden hand looms specially made by Arrol Young in Scotland. Yarn was no longer to be spun 'in-house' but bought in and, as a result, the spinning and carding machinery on the ground floor was mothballed.

The main conundrum for Bob was the amount of time it takes to train a hand loom weaver. At that time he was the only person in the mill qualified to weave on a hand loom. Some of his weavers had had to be laid off and the small number remaining, who had been trained up to work the power looms in just a matter of months, now needed a four year apprenticeship to learn completely new techniques.

By April 1963, however, there was no going back. Worldwide publicity brought in a welcome stream of orders from a wide variety of countries such as Kuwait, Bermuda and Scandinavia [6]. Within a year the mill was employing 25 workers and manufacturing tweeds, worsteds and knitting wools from blended Manx, New Zealand and Australian wools [7]. As the decade unfolded the weavers met their new challenge with vigour, another four

Advert for Arrol Young hand looms

Bob Wood weaving on a bedstead 4-treadle cantilever hand loom, made by Arrol Young

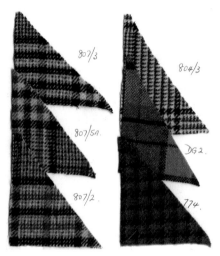

A 1960s Laxey mill pattern book, sent on request

A 1960s brochure

St. George's Woollen Mills

(Founded by John Ruskin in 1881)

Exclusive ★

HANDWOVEN

★ Manx Tweeds

A CORDIAL INVITATION is extended to all Holidaymakers to visit the Mills and see the Hand-Loom Unit in Operation

" HORSE POWER WAS SAFER WHEN THE HORSES HAD IT "

(Extract from "The Wool Record and Textile World")

★ See the Old-Time Skill which has survived for Centuries

Branches at: Castle Street, Douglas; Strand Road, Port Erin, and Manx Electric Railway Station, Laxey. Telephones: Port Erin Branch: Port Erin 3027; Mills: Laxey 395; Douglas Branch: Douglas 3150

"It hardly looks like the modern conception of a woollen mill. But hand-weaving is a gentle industry and at Laxey the factory floor is a showroom for tourists as well"
(IOM Examiner Jan 30th 1964)

power looms were disposed of and two more hand looms were brought in, plus a domestic pedal loom. As well as managing the mill, designing fabrics and training his staff, Bob himself became one of the mill's main weavers. Before long a large shop area was created alongside the weaving machinery on the first floor so that customers could watch him and his team at work.

Before the Sixties were over three-quarters of the mill's output was handwoven and they had secured much sought after business from Canada and America. On the domestic front, the TT and Grand Prix races brought in steady streams of enthusiastic new customers and during race time Bob and Sally capitalised on this by hiring out tartan rugs to spectators at Creg-ny-Baa. The mill was also entrusted with the spinning and weaving of the wool from the Manx Loaghtan sheep reared by the Manx museum [8] and they produced Loaghtan tweed as part of their souvenir lines. To the family's, and board of directors, relief it seemed that Bob's gamble was paying off.

Once the mill's new routine began to prove successful the Wood family were able to buy a house on Pinfold Hill on the outskirts of Laxey village and young John and Dian attended Laxey School. After school the children would go down to the mill and often spend time in the mending room where they'd sit beneath the tables on pieces of cloth and be fussed over by the mill girls. By the age of eight they were given small jobs to do such as working the cheese winder (so named because a 'cheese' of wool is the end product). They tried to avoid the weaving room though as the remaining power looms produced tremendous noise and vibration which was terrifying to a small child! On weekends they were expected to help with cleaning and rubbish collection and when they weren't needed in the mill they were allowed to play outdoors on the 'deads' or down by the river.

For a few years the Wood family routine settled into one of long, hard days but gradually increasing rewards. Then in September 1967 everything changed. A fire broke out in the mill one night causing the yarn and cloth to smoulder, creating a pall of thick black smoke which was intensified by oil and grease from the machinery. The Fire Brigade used water to prevent the fire spreading but it caused the idle carding and spinning machinery to go rusty virtually overnight.

The company's only choice was to hold a massive 'fire sale' and over a period of just three days villagers descended on the mill to buy up the entire stock of smoke-damaged wool and fabric. A local carrier came down and took away the damaged spinning and carding machinery and the Woods then had to decide what to do with the now-empty ground floor. This time the answer was simple. The mill's days as a purely manufacturing concern were effectively over and it seemed logical to convert the ground floor into a retail unit. Used roofing felt was used to line the floor, counters were quickly put up and stock bought in. A whole new sales department soon sprang up, complete with hand loom, and the rest of the building was given a much-needed facelift. But this was also the heyday of the mill's retail outlets at Port Erin, Douglas, Ramsey and the Laxey MER station and in an extraordinary turnaround of fortunes the St George's Mill company experienced a 'record summer'.

Their newfound success came at a price however. In 1968, one of the St George's Woollen Mills directors, wealthy Liverpool businessman Michael Higgin, forced a buy-out of the mill and its subsidiaries. But the takeover was short-lived. The following year the Woods bought the entire shareholding of St George's Woollen Mills land, buildings, plant, stock and machinery and it has remained in the sole ownership of the family ever since. This was a huge turning point for Bob and Sally, entailing massive commitment, but it also meant that after years of being accountable to shareholders they could run the business how they wanted. And it paid off. Towards the end of 1969 a local newspaper article reported that an estimated 50,000 visitors had passed through the doors of the mill in that year alone![9]

Now Bob and May Brew were the main weavers and they needed to weave thousands of yards of fabric each season to keep up with demand. Many of the visitors who poured out of the coaches at the mill were workers from the big car factories in the Midlands. They were good customers with plenty of ready cash and they bought up knitwear, overcoats, tweed jackets, lengths of fabric, knick-knacks and souvenirs. Exports of handwoven goods were also taking off with many 'urgent orders' for Canada and New York. The ever-important American market was going through important stylistic changes at this time and the mill needed to keep up. American buyers liked the 'rustic' look but insisted on lightweight tweeds as, even in the middle of winter, they could rely on heated cars and centrally heated buildings. The mill was also discovering that different countries had different colour preferences. In America and Australia the preferred tones were brown-tone tweed while the Germans preferred blue, grey and green [10].

Success for the mill – and their ownership of the business after years of being accountable to shareholders – brought about a new dynamic in Bob and Sally's relationship. While he concentrated on the manufacturing side, Sally was full of ideas and had a keen eye for new products and style trends. They started attending trade shows in Scotland and experimenting with new lines such as suede outfits, full-length women's kilts and sheepskin car-seat covers.

Coachtours and Cafes

In the Sixties the Isle of Man began competing with the exciting new package holidays to Europe and had to work hard to keep up. A major step forward was the launching, in 1962, of the Island's first car ferry 'Manx Maid'. This opened up a whole new opportunity for visitors to bring their own transport and drive around the Island at their own free will. Before long it was noted that Laxey was the perfect destination for an afternoon outing as it could be 'conveniently visited within the intervals between the mealtimes of the boarding houses.'

Coach trips were also becoming popular with comfortable little coaches replacing the earlier open charabancs. Bob and Sally Wood saw huge opportunities for the Laxey mill in this new trend and in the quiet early spring of 1965 they worked hard to refurbish the mill's retail showroom-cum-weaving floor. As the summer unfolded they would then take regular trips into Douglas to 'sell' the mill to the coach drivers. At the height of the season Sally even spent afternoons on Port Erin promenade tempting coach drivers to head north with the promise of tea, biscuits and half a crown. Their tactics paid off. The coach business soon became so important to the success of the mill that those drivers that included it on their tour itineraries were often 'rewarded' with bottles of whisky and vodka!

The first coaches to visit the mill were Manx coaches run by Fred Kelly. His passengers were often weavers or factory workers from Lancashire, Yorkshire and Ireland and although they weren't big spenders it was a start and word began to spread about the mill as a new Laxey attraction. Some companies even began taking their visitors on 'mystery tours' which usually took place at the end of the day. On a number of occasions the Wood family would be enjoying a quiet evening at home when the cry "coach tour!" would go up and Bob and Sally would rush down to open up the mill.

"In the summer months between 18 and 25 coaches would sometimes come to the mill in one morning! Then between 2.30 and 4 in the afternoon another 10 to 15 coaches would turn up. They'd be parked all the way down the Glen Road".
(John Wood)

The advent of the coach tour customer meant a gradual shift in the type of products on sale in the mill shop towards the souvenir market. Bob was still weaving and developing the hand looms while May Brew worked on the power looms but production was more or less confined to handwoven Manx tweeds for skirt length packs. After the fire of 1967 and subsequent refurbishment the Laxey mill became almost totally geared towards the visitor market. The holiday season was still dictated by Wakes Weeks, the 'staggered' system of holidays for different industries, and it meant for busy times as hundreds of people descended on the mill at any one time. During the summer holidays the mill regularly employed many young local teenagers.

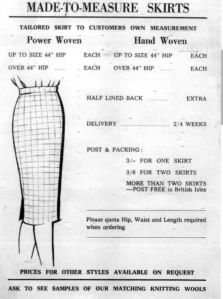

To give their customers added value Bob and Sally decided to set up a small tearoom in the mill. This was located just inside the back entrance, on the site of the old dye house. A kitchen was set up in the adjoining room, which also doubled as a canteen for coach drivers and mill employees, and a serving hatch connected the two. The kitchen had formerly been used as the mill shop but this was no longer needed thanks to the new retail area within the main building.

The tearoom was basic but cheerful in a Sixties sort of way, furnished with yellow formica tables and matching yellow chairs. Here visitors could enjoy a cup of tea and a ham bap or tub of Manx ice cream before piling back into their coaches and cars, loaded up with handwoven rugs and knitting wool. Ice cream was also dispensed to passing visitors through the kitchen doorway that opened onto the Glen Road.

"When I was fifteen or sixteen I spent a whole summer running the mill tearoom and loved it. It was incredibly busy with one coach after another, but it was a very happy place. Mr Wood was always clattering away on the loom and Mrs Wood was highly organised, seeing to customers and making sure everything ran smoothly. May, the other weaver, was my Sunday School teacher and she made me feel really welcome."
Jean Halsall (nee Caley), Mill employee circa 1968

Advertisement in All About Mann, 1974

Trading seasons for the mill settled into a steady pattern of peaks and troughs. From March older customers would come in to buy tweed suits and traditional lengths of cloth. Then the arrival of motorcycle fans during TT fortnight in June always saw a huge upsurge of travel rug and souvenir sales as they snapped up anything that would fit in a pannier – from tea towels to tapestry sets. The Manx Grand Prix was also good for business but this came at the end of the summer and signalled the end of the season. By late September the mill would fall quiet again. In October the whole business closed down for annual staff holidays and the Wood family headed to Blackpool for a well-earned rest. The dark winter months that followed were used for mending cloth set aside from the previous summer.

In 1978, with the Manx Millennium approaching and Paddy McQuaid's Manx tartan no longer available, Bob decided to design a new Manx-themed tartan using just five colours – blue, yellow, green, purple and white. The tartan was registered with the Scottish Tartan Society as the Laxey Manx Tartan and quickly became one of the mill's biggest sellers.

THE LAXEY MANX TARTAN

with

The Blue for the Sea,
Green for the Hills,
Gold for the Gorse,
Purple for the Heather
and
White for the Cottages.

A section of the Laxey Manx tartan designed by Bob Wood

In 1979 the family's hard work finally paid off. The Mill was granted a special licence to produce a Barathea tie with the Millennium symbol; sales of all their products reached new highs and the Seventies ended on the best year of the decade.

A Touch of Luxury

Despite the explosion of 'shocking' fashions in the Sixties the St George's Mill remained true to its traditional roots and continued to produce goods aimed at the conventional customer. Bob Wood was always insistent on quality and only ever wanted the best in pure new wool, refusing to buy in any synthetic fabrics or yarns from outside Britain. Smart indoor and outdoor wear in tweed, mohair, wool and cashmere were their main lines with a regular stock list of stoles (a type of ladies wrap), scarves, gloves, pram rugs, cot blankets, knee and travel rugs, ties, skirt lengths, jumpers and twinsets. A typical mill customer would usually be seen wearing gloves and a hat and this continued until the advent of the coach tripper who was more casually dressed. Lengths of cloth for men's suits virtually disappeared in the early Sixties. Women continued to have their clothing made up privately, but many small tailors had gone out of business and men's suits could now be easily purchased off-the-peg from large clothing stores.

Laxey woollen mill goods were sold throughout the Island, from the village Post Office to a small wooden hut on Strand Road in Port Erin. Port Erin was similar to Ramsey during the Sixties and Seventies with many thriving hotels and guest houses, sandy beaches, an open air swimming pool, folk dances and hotel dances. The Strand Road shop was run by Mrs Ingles and Mrs Corrin. It was only a tiny building on what is a grassy area below Falcon Cliff, but was perfectly placed to catch the droves of holidaymakers making their way from the Railway Station to the beach. The hut was demolished in the mid-Sixties and the business was moved across the road to a two storey shop building with large windows facing the street. This remained open into the next decade.

In Douglas, the Castle Street shop, run by Mrs Hulley, was a two storey affair in the heart of what was a thriving commercial part of town, made up largely of old-established family businesses. Here the woollen mills shop sat comfortably alongside Fred Brew the Butcher, Curpheys – originally a plumbers business then

Did you know?

Merino wool is a fine, high quality wool from the Australian merino sheep. Shetland is super-soft wool from a particular breed of British sheep.

gift and shoe shops, Corlett the Jewellers and Kermode and Bignell shoe retailers, plus smaller shops selling linen and lace, ice cream, fresh fish and sweet Manx 'rock'.

These were great times for retailers but once Strand Street was pedestrianised in 1977 and large multiples opened at the other end of town small businesses began to struggle. After Mrs Hulley retired, rising rents and staffing problems put pressure on the mill shop but with business going so well in Laxey there was no longer any real need for it. In 1979 it was closed down and shortly after the building was demolished to make way for the Tower House shopping centre.

The Sixties saw the mill's relationship with prestigious local hotels blossom. Well-to-do holidaymakers with extra disposable income were keen to buy the mill's high quality, 'country-style' clothing, golf wear and distinctive gifts. In 1968 the Castletown Golf Links Hotel displayed the mill goods in a glass cabinet in the foyer, including ladies twin sets, Monaco jumpers, mohair travel rugs and head squares. At the adjoining Golf shop sporting visitors wanting to add a touch of flair to their on-course outfits could purchase smaller items such as tweed golf caps and woollen scarves.

By the Seventies the mill's range extended to car coats and sports jackets, and when the fabric department was moved upstairs a new section was opened purely for suede suits and sheepskin coats, the suede suits scoring an immediate hit with female customers. These were seen as stylish, classy and modern. Even home knitting was given a Seventies makeover with a new trend for fancy yarns such as bouclés.

The Revival of Handicrafts

In the Seventies the dwindling tourism scene in the Isle of Man was a major concern for Island retailers and the visiting industry. In 1979 though, the Island was due to celebrate the Millennium of Tynwald and this was seen as a big opportunity to 'sell' the Isle of Man on the international stage. Integral to its success was a renewed enthusiasm for Manx culture which had started in the late Sixties. This was reflected in a revival of traditional handicrafts and it was fortunate for the Laxey Woollen mill that their hand loom ethos fitted well into this creative way of thinking. During the Sixties the mill was even opened up to school trips with primary school children invited to come and watch Bob weave.

'The revival of interest in ancient crafts of spinning, weaving and dyeing reflect not only a desire for individuality in an increasingly uniform world but a growing appreciation of the qualities of natural materials and the craftsmanship that can create something unique.'
('Spinning, Dyeing and Weaving – A WI Home Skills Guide', WI Books Ltd. 1979)

In 1971 the Isle of Man Crafts Association was set up to encourage Manx arts and crafts. Handcrafted souvenirs became all the rage – artisans around the Island

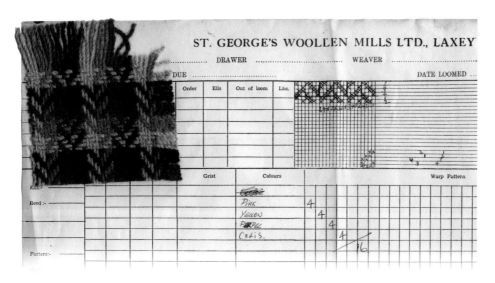

A 1970s 'piece ticket', giving the weaver the required pattern and colours.

EXCLUSIVE
HANDWOVEN
MANX TWEEDS

A CORDIAL INVITATION is extended to all Holidaymakers
to visit the Mills and see the Hand-Loom unit in operation

For Sale in our Showrooms:—
**Manx Tweeds, Mohairs, Sheepskin, Deerskin and
Suede Products of quality**

See the Old-Time Skill which has survived for Centuries
St. George's Woollen Mills Ltd.
Founded by John Ruskin in 1881

Open 10 a.m. to 6 p.m. —— MONDAY to SATURDAY

*The idea of weaving while
wearing a suit is long gone!*

offered a range of woodwork, pottery, basketry and shellwork and on a more commercial scale Kelly's Souvenirs at Jurby supplied miniature thatched cottages and other iconic Manx mementoes.

A publication even started up to support this new movement. The first issue of 'Manninagh' featured an article on spinning, dyeing and weaving and the second recounted the story of George 'Juan Y Fidder' Corkhill from Ballaglass, the last in a long line of cottage hand loom weavers who had lived at the Dullan, Maughold since the 1700s [11].

It didn't take long for advertising companies to take up the 'handicrafts' baton and in the Sixties and Seventies the Laxey mill was more than happy to push its image as a 'charming rural industry'. In 1971 a full page advert and poster produced for the mill shows a man in a suit working on a hand loom producing 'exclusive handwoven Manx Tweeds'.

The Weaver's Apprentice

For John Wood life had always been entwined with the Laxey Woollen Mill. Right from an early age his family life revolved around it, both parents lived and breathed it, and it was perhaps inevitable that one day he would step into his father's shoes and become a Laxey weaver. But it didn't always seem that way. For John, the great passion in his early life was sport. As a boy he was always the youngest and smallest in his class and often got into scrapes but on moving to St Ninian's High School he found he could immerse himself in sport, in particular rugby which he loved and played well. As a teenager growing up in Laxey he and his close band of friends would also spend any free time fishing, cycling and exploring.

Not that he had much free time. By the age of 12 or 13 John and his sister Dian were each given a loom and some simple instruction in weaving. A year or so later he got a holiday job working for Harold Corlett the local butcher, where he helped to make dripping and sterilise the shop. He also spent some time at Manx Engineers and began to take on more responsible jobs in the mill doing lower skilled jobs and working in the yarn store. Then, in the spring of 1974, when John finished his GCSEs, Bob Wood asked him if he would like to work in the mill on a proper footing and with that John began a five year apprenticeship working five days a week.

To begin with his father taught him the basics of design and how to weave and warp, and during that first summer John worked continually on a Hattersley Domestic Pedal Loom, similar to the type used by the Harris tweed industry. A pedal loom is operated by the feet with a cycling motion and for the whole of the rest of the summer John steadily pedalled away. But it was extremely hard work and physically draining and by the end of the year his father was persuaded to fit the loom with a motor!

The following January John, by then aged 16, was sent to work for a few months in a mill in Selkirk which specialised in making high quality gents tartan kilt lengths. Here he found new inspiration and soaked up everything he was taught, including how to set up looms. He also worked for a short time at Andrew Stewart's in Galashiels, world famous for making high quality mohair products. On returning to the Isle of Man he was even more determined to become a weaver and soon began a four year sandwich course at his father's old college, the Scottish College of Textiles. This meant spending time working in the Laxey mill during the busy Millennium Year and it proved to be a turning point. John was given his own responsibilities and worked the Hattersley upstairs while his father worked the hand loom downstairs. John's presence brought youth and colour to the old mill and his future direction became increasingly apparent.

A short time later Bob Wood wrote to a friend *'It is still a hard slog during the season. Six days a week working from April to October is getting ridiculous at my time of life'* [12].

It was time for a new pair of hands at the loom. The apprentice was ready and waiting.

References:

1. 'A 1962 Guide to the Isle of Man' Qualyfoto, Castle Mona shops, Douglas
2. 'The Isle of Man – A Study In Economic Geography' J.W. Birch, Cambridge University Press 1964
3. Laxey Guide 1970s p.20
4. Pauline Weston Thomas www.fashion-era.com
5. IOM Examiner 30th January 1964, MNH
6. IOM Weekly Times 26th April 1963, MNH
7. Birch ibid. p.169
8. IOM Weekly Times 31st October 1969, MNH
9. ibid
10. Wool Record, September 1978 p.35
11. Constance Radcliffe 'Manninagh' No.2 1972 p.88, private collection
12. Bob Wood to Tom Mylchreest, letter dated 27th August 1977

CHAPTER SEVEN
1980 - 2000

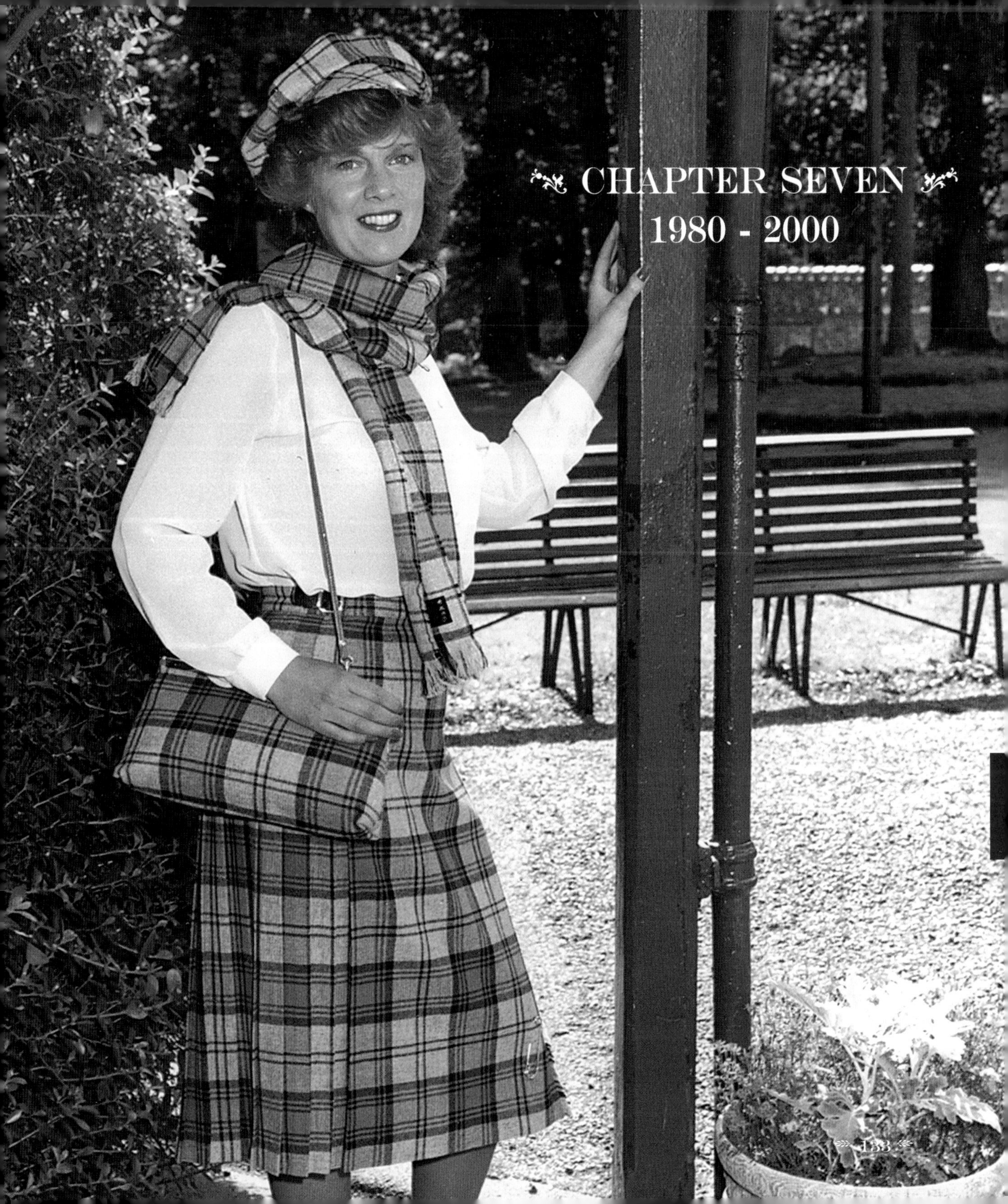

Timeline

1981	The Royal Wedding of Prince Charles and Lady Diana Spencer
1982	Inaugural flight of Manx Airlines
1985	The Wheel Café totally destroyed by fire
1985	Visit to Laxey by Princess Alexandra
1986	First 'Duck Race' held at Easter in the Laxey river
1987	Laxey Heritage Trust established (taken over by the Laxey & Lonan Heritage Trust in 1997)
1989-92	First Gulf War
1993	The Isle of Man formally abolishes capital punishment
1994	Heavy snow in February causes the closure of schools
1994	Laxey's Christmas Torchlight procession held for the first time
1994	Palace Lido demolished
1997	Princess Diana killed in a car accident in Paris
1998	Manx National Heritage acquires Rushen Abbey
1999	Laxey School extension opened

Bob Wood's grandson Robert in the Laxey mill

Holidays & High Finance

Families from the North West of England have been visiting the Isle of Man in their thousands ever since the mid-nineteenth century and for many years virtually held the monopoly. By the late 1980s, however, they only accounted for a third of the total visitors to the Island as people came from further afield and for reasons other than sandy beaches and pretty glens. The Island's beaches were still as beautiful as ever but with warmer destinations providing stiff competition the tourist board had to turn the spotlight on a more diverse range of attractions to try and boost the dwindling number of holidaymakers reaching Manx shores.

The general downturn of the tourist industry had a serious knock-on effect on the whole Manx economy and in the Eighties the Government had to take swift action to redress the balance. Financial and tax incentives were introduced in a bid to encourage new businesses and wealthy individuals to relocate to the Island, and before long the growth of the finance and banking sector was putting the Isle of Man on the map as a respected offshore financial centre. By the end of the twentieth century the deckchairs that once crowded Douglas beach were few and far between, even on hot sunny days, and many of the capital's hotels and boarding houses were converted to offices and apartments.

In the mid-Nineties though the Island began to enjoy a new swing towards holidays marketed in terms of culture, sport, adventure, transport, nostalgia or family history and visitor numbers reached almost half a million. There was also a noticeable shift to the rural heart of the Island where farm stays, self-catering cottages and specialist guest houses began to thrive. Many modern visitors bring their own cars or travel in comfortable, air-conditioned coaches and enjoy independent holidays rather than the group affairs of old. The pleasure of travelling by vintage tram and train has changed very little but in the Eighties and Nineties families were just as likely to walk the coastal and Millennium pathways or take sea excursions to look out for dolphins and basking sharks.

'Stroll through picturesque Laxey Glen Gardens where you can enjoy refreshments at the kiosk by the Wild Fowl Lake. Find out more about Laxey and our summer programme, including bands, dances, sheepdog trials, craft demonstrations etc.'
(Laxey Heritage Trust advert SeaWatch Aug-Sept 1988)

Laxey — "A Working Victorian Masterpiece"

The establishment of the Laxey Heritage Trust in the 1980s was a major step forward for the village, rekindling it as a tourist destination. In 1987 they set up an information centre, guided tours of local beauty and historical interest spots and produced trail leaflets. Events were held regularly in the Laxey Glen Gardens on Sundays in the Trust's first year, and workshops for a blacksmith and wood carver were established near to the station. Restoration work was carried out on the Laxey Wheel.

In the late Eighties Manx tourism bosses took the promotion of Laxey's heritage a step further by touting the village as 'a working Victorian masterpiece'[1]. Aside from the Victorian engineering marvel that is the Laxey Wheel visitors could now also explore a restored section of the mine tunnels and continue their 'Victorian experience' with 'working treasures' such as the flour mills, pipe works, tram station and glen gardens. And, of course, the St George's Woollen mills.

Bob Wood loading a weaving shuttle

During the Eighties and Nineties a number of special dates on the calendar became the subject of new community enthusiasm. Easter, Harvest festivals and Hop-tu-Naa have always been well celebrated in Laxey, but during these years they also became the focus for fund-raising events marked by dressing up and 'family fun'. A good example is the Great Laxey Duck Race, when thousands of yellow plastic ducks are released into the river with prizes on offer for the first ducks over the line. Over the years the event has grown into a serious fund-raiser which draws hundreds of onlookers.

A ripple of excitement gripped the village in the mid-Nineties when 'showbiz came to town'. The old power station/carpet factory on Glen Road was converted into a film studio as part of the Manx Government's push to encourage film makers and for a while residents became quite used to seeing famous faces such as Daniel Craig and Billy Piper on the street. The most notable films to be shot partly in Laxey included 'Waking Ned', 'The Tichbourne Claimant', 'Alice Through the Looking Glass' and 'Darkness Falls'.

What Shall I Wear Today?

The new found confidence of women in the workplace gave rise to a worldwide fashion phenomenon in the Eighties known as 'power dressing'. This was mainly indicated by the use of shoulder pads which became bigger and more outrageous as the decade progressed. Television dramas from the United States almost gave shoulder pads a role all of their own in the likes of 'Dynasty' and 'Dallas' where the female leads (all glamorous, powerful women) wore shoulder pads under their suits, blouses, evening gowns and knitwear. But for all their comedy value now most ordinary women loved shoulder pads as they made clothes hang well and made hips appear slimmer!

For working women power dressing was gradually translated into more subtle corporate wear. Smart, tailored suits, trousers or pencil skirts in dark colours, especially black, soon became the uniform of the office worker. Many garments were manufactured in lightweight synthetic fabrics such as polyester, but wool or wool mixes have remained in constant use for women's suiting right through to the twenty-first century.

KNITTING CATALOGUE

Knitted in Luxury Mohair
see pages 10 & 11
for details

for
SPRING
& SUMMER
1988

● readicut

The biggest fashion icon of the 1980s was undoubtedly Princess Diana. Women the world over soon began to follow and imitate her every fashion move, from small pillbox hats to low heeled shoes and wide lace collars. In her early married life she was often seen wearing tweed clothing for her forays to the Royal country residences but even gave these a new feminine twist, having the jackets tailored 'bomber style' or given gathered shoulders.

Diana helped give a boost to knitwear in the Eighties, wearing the distinctive styles of the decade such as cowl neck jumpers and batwing

John Wood operating a Hattersley Domestic hand loom

sleeves. Even knitted jumpers had shoulder pads. By the '90s these were attached with Velcro so they could be removed if the garment was being worn underneath a similarly padded jacket. The large knitted shawl, often decorated with a Liberty pattern, was a popular accessory, often worn with plain business suits or jackets to soften the overall look.

The range of woollen clothing produced by Laxey Woollen Mills in the Eighties leaned towards elegant sweaters, cardigans, skirts and jackets in a range of patterns and plains, checks and tweeds. But in contrast to the Eighties' trend for bold, bright colours, the colours employed in the mill were kept deliberately soft with names such as blue ice, soft jade, heatherlie, rose quartz and tourmaline.

Tartan enjoyed a prominent role in the Eighties female wardrobe, manifested as shawls, skirts and scarves. In 1981 the Laxey Woollen Mill scored an instant hit with their 'Centenary tartan' marking the mill's one hundred year anniversary. This was designed by Bob Wood and incorporated grey, duck egg blue, blue and dark blue. The grey was intended to represent the original grey flannel woven in the Ruskin era, and the blue and green were derived from the ever popular Laxey Manx Tartan[2]. Other Manx themed tartans were also produced at that time including the Ellan Vannin (green), Snaefell (brown and cream) and the Laksaa (black and white).

Centenary tartan

Ellan Vannin tartan

Snaefell Tartan

Casual wear was definitely becoming the norm, however, seen in the growth of cheap, easy-to-wear garments such as cotton sweatshirts. Similarly, casual outdoor wear was also increasingly popular to complement the Eighties emphasis on health and fitness. And the decade marked a turning point in children's wear. Up until then children were expected to wear whatever their parents dressed them in (usually home-knitted pullovers, homemade dresses and structured clothing) but suddenly there were dedicated children's fashion ranges, jeans and trainers, and youngsters were given more freedom of choice in what they wore.

After the sharp focus of the Eighties, clothing in the Nineties seemed to have some of the stuffing knocked out of it. Maybe it was a reaction to a decade of clearly defined trends but this period had a much more dressed-down feel and many fashions from previous eras re-appeared in new guises. Knitwear for younger women was often worn in the form of long sweaters over tight leggings and long cardigans began to replace jackets or coats. For the more mature woman the smart woollen blazer became a staple item but could be worn equally well with tailored skirts and trousers or jeans. Once again Lady Diana was influential in this respect. Chain stores became the norm, factory outlets sprang up and second-hand clothing took on a new respectability.

> **Did you know?**
> *Wool that is compacted into felt becomes even more water resistant and long-wearing. Felt is used in felt-tip pens, polishing wheels, felt hats, tennis ball covers and felt yurts — traditional tents used by nomadic Eastern Europeans.*

The Mill beyond the Manx Millennium

After the halcyon days of the Manx Millennium in 1979 and subsequent couple of years, it seemed the Laxey Woollen mills were in for a good spell. John was now working as a full-time hand loom weaver, along with his father and May Brew, and orders began to arrive from the most unexpected places. In the early Eighties they even received a request from the Hong Kong Police Pipe Band for large quantities of Laxey Manx tartan! The Chief of Police at the time happened to be a Manxman and struck on the idea of using his own national tartan to dress the band. Hundreds of metres of cloth were despatched to Hong Kong where they were made up into trews, capes, glengarries and used on their bagpipes.

Hong Kong Police Pipe Band wearing Laxey Manx Tartan

Then, almost without warning, Manx tourism nosedived and business suddenly became hard again.

All of the Mill's out-of-town retail outlets were closed down and sales were only made from the mill or the small shop run by Olive Ingham at the Laxey Manx Electric Railway station. This shop was directly geared towards visitors stepping off the trams from Ramsey and Douglas and sold plenty of small, portable clothing items and souvenirs such as purses and ties made, for the first time, out of the Laxey Manx tartan.

A turning point came in the mid-Eighties when the mill joined seven other specialist Manx industries in a delegation to the International Giftware Fair in Birmingham[3]. The publicity was invaluable and helped them secure some all-important American orders, particularly for a distinctive rose and purple tweed which satisfied the transatlantic desire for bold new colours. The Fair also gave Sally Wood an important introduction to representatives from the giant firm of Liberty[4]. Liberty's distinctive style was very popular in the Eighties and Sally felt their giftware would complement the mill's core woven products. Before long the mill had an exclusive deal with Liberty to sell their woollen skirt fabrics, tote bags, picture frames, purses, shopping bags and 'beanie' frogs.

Sally Wood

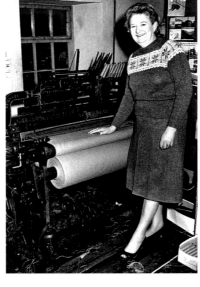

The Liberty stand in the Laxey Woollen mills, 1983

"With designer knitwear as diverse and famous as Tulchan amongst others, Liberty of London giftware. With quality wool products ranging in price from two pounds to two hundred pounds, offering value, style, warmth and comfort; with a range of Manx tartan gift ideas from ties to rugs, hats to scarves and a worldwide mail service; with loads of easy parking and gift ideas; without doubt we're talking about Laxey Woollen Mills in Glen Road, Laxey"
(Manx Radio commercial, circa 1985)

1988 Mill employees wearing Laxey Manx tartan

*Bob Wood had
weaving in his fingertips*

In 1988 Bob Wood officially retired, although he would often come in to the mill for a few hours a day to work alongside John. Despite his advancing years he still liked to have the upper hand and would deliberately weave faster than his son to show there was life in the old dog yet!

'Today the Mill's speciality is a co-ordinated range of Manx Tweeds... made up of 78 beautiful mixture shades such as Blue Ice, Dolphin, Fuchsia, Sea Turquoise, Bilberry, Geronal etc. You can see these being woven so you know they are genuine.' (Manx Independent July 1990)

In the mid-nineties a quarter of the mill's output was sold off-Island although they made a conscious decision to aim at smaller American outlets than in previous years, such as those geared towards specialist lines like cashmere blankets and Celtic products. Wealthy American individuals also proved to be good customers, such as the president of the Cadillac motor company who regularly ordered mohair travelling rugs for Christmas gifts.

Purple tones were very popular

Closer to home, Bob observed that the British market was changing dramatically with all his old retailers being bought out by large groups who operated central buying.

In 1995 the Manx Government established the Isle of Man Film Commission to encourage filmmakers to use the Island's diverse locations and studio facilities. Laxey was able to offer both and this brought some interesting custom for the Woollen Mill. During a remake of 'Treasure Island' a tall, imposing man dressed in American hat and boots came into the mill to look at the Manx tartans. The minute he spoke everyone immediately recognised Hollywood star Jack Palance who was playing the role of Long John Silver in the film. In between shoots he and his wife were keen to get a flavour of the Isle of Man and this small taste of showbiz was the talk of the mill for weeks to come, although over the next few years Laxey folk became quite blasé about the number of famous faces wandering around the village!

But it wasn't only the stars of the films who supported local businesses. On a number of occasions the Woollen Mill was required to supply the film makers with yards of tartan fabric to dress both sets and actors.

In 1995 the leading American performance artist Matthew Barney incorporated Laxey Manx tartan in an art video called 'Cremaster 4' shot on the Isle of Man. Not in the conventional sense however – these tartan scarves were worn by strange blue leather-clad faeries with bright red hair! Barney himself played a satyr called the Loughtan Candidate and the film is full of Manx references such as the TT, Faeries and the Three Legs.

Video artist Matthew Barney against a backdrop of Laxey Manx tartan

Manx tartan kilts, jackets, serapes, shawls, tam o shanters, trilbys, rugs, mohair scarves and stoles, skirts, purses, glasses cases, hats, ties, socks, the loaghtyn range of sweaters, ties, skirts, cloth, knitting wools, lightweight coats and scarves, slippers, gloves, knitwear, blouses, sweatshirts, children's clothing, Shetland items, purses, paper, travel rugs, souvenirs, soft toys, cufflinks, key rings, Liberty items, yarn and cloth.
(Stock list of 1990s products sold in the Mill)

The old St George's Woollen Mills buildings still maintained an air of solid tradition, however, and physically their appearance and purpose remained fairly constant during the latter years of the twentieth century. Even the remains of the old defunct tenter frames could still be seen on the embankment until the mid-Nineties when they finally disappeared into the undergrowth. The building was starting to feel its age – but perhaps a relatively quiet period wasn't such a bad thing. The challenges of a new era were waiting just around the corner.

References:
1. 1989 Official Isle of Man holiday brochure, IoM Tourist Board.
2. www.tartanregister.gov.uk
3. IOM Examiner 8th October 1986.
4. IOM Examiner 18th December 1985

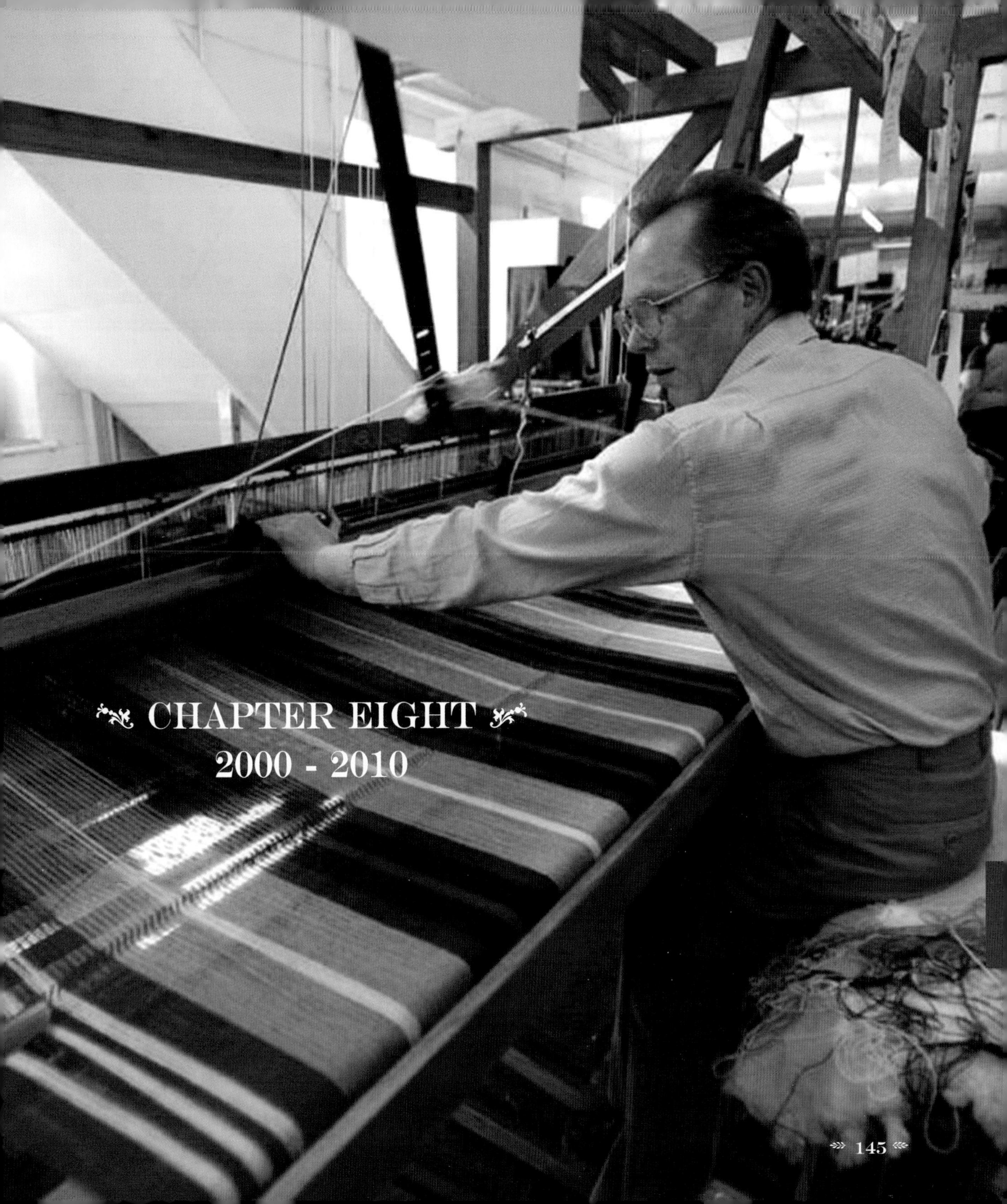

CHAPTER EIGHT
2000 - 2010

Timeline

2000 Millennium Year

2002 Heavy rainfall and high tides cause severe flooding and landslips in Laxey. A number of properties were damaged

2003 Old Noble's Hospital closes. New Noble's Hospital opens at the Strang

2004 150th anniversary of the Laxey Wheel

2005 Flood lighting installed in the Laxey Valley Gardens

2006 Official opening of the restored Snaefell wheel, 'Lady Evelyn', in the Valley Gardens

2006 Formal opening of the Laxey Heritage Trail

2007 Centenary of the TT motorcycle races

Laxey looking towards South Cape

Laxey in the Twenty First Century

On the surface, twenty-first century Laxey may no longer appear to be the self-contained hamlet it once was. Many of the families living in the area have occupations based in other towns and very few people do all their shopping in the village. But look deeper and it's not hard to find the strong sense of community that Laxey has always been proud of. The Post Office is still the hub of the village and some activities such as football, keep fit and social get togethers have barely changed in a hundred years. But there are also plenty of modern pastimes to take advantage of – from yoga to skateboarding. John Wood is himself a leading member of the successful district rifle club and young people have a huge range of organised activities to choose from, led largely by Laxey School and local youth and church groups.

Enjoying a drink!

Social life is as important as ever to maintaining the heart of the village whether it takes the form of pubs, fairs or concerts. The annual Fair, held in the Valley Gardens on a warm summer evening, always attracts a good turnout, giving local children (and some adults!) the chance to dress up in Victorian clothing, follow the band and sing traditional songs. Then there are garden competitions, frequent table top sales and charity events which always draw keen support.

One of Laxey's most enduring draw cards is its natural beauty and thankfully, the look of the village has been mostly maintained in the new century. The Glen Gardens are quieter than at any time in their history but the beech trees are just as magnificent and the walkways and river offer their own, peaceful attractions. Throughout the village many original cottages have been carefully restored and, although modern residential developments have sprung up on the outskirts of Laxey, the centre of the village is now largely protected by Conservation Area status. Shops and businesses come and go but there is still a wide variety of retailers to cater for most daily needs.

Celebrating the Victorian era at Laxey Fair

*Laxey's most famous landmark,
the great Laxey Wheel*

Snaefell Mountain Railway

The rhythms of modern Laxey life are dictated mostly by the seasons. Winter is traditionally very quiet (apart from the somewhat unconventional arrival of Santa in a lifeboat!). But in the summer, when the trams are running, the village comes to life as thousands of visitors descend on the area to enjoy its scenery, history and seaside, just as they did in the 1800s. Trips to the summit of Snaefell are as popular as ever and the newly revamped promenade continues to attract crowds of holidaymakers and – during TT fortnight – hundreds of bikes!

Culture in Laxey is alive and kicking. The area where young boys used to wash lead ore is now the perfect venue for visiting outdoor theatre companies; local concerts are always popular and a number of artists and craftspeople find inspiration in the valley's environs.

Many residents are also keen to preserve and celebrate the area's rich and diverse history and their efforts often make the headlines. The work done by volunteers on the Snaefell 'Lady Evelyn' Wheel and the restored Great Laxey Mine railway brings in hundreds of visitors to the Valley Gardens every year and in recent years the Laxey Mines Research Group have undertaken a number of restoration projects. The Laxey & Lonan Heritage Trust is more active than ever in promoting the history of the village. Boat trips on the steamer MV Karina, guided walks, talks and socials frequently bring together a wide section of the population.

The Laxey Working Men's Institute on New Road has also had new life breathed into it. After decades of standing idle and neglected, a local working party of energetic volunteers has raised funds and contributed their own labour to restoring this historic building. As this book goes to press it is hoped the Institute will soon be resounding once more to the sound of happy village voices.

A 21st Century Mill

Against this background, the St George's Woollen Mill has continued to evolve. In 2000 Sally Wood died at the age of sixty-one after a lifetime dedicated to the mill. Even when she was seriously ill she refused to slow down, insisting on having catalogues and paperwork brought to her in hospital. Sally's death left a big gap in the day-to-day life of the mill and for the next few years things fell very quiet. As Bob's health was also failing John was left to pretty much manage the business on his own. Despite his poor health though Bob could never face the thought of retiring and 'lived and breathed' the mill to the very end, spending most of his days sitting in a corner of the Gent's Department. On Christmas Eve 2006 he passed away, aged 82.

The Laxey Woollen Mills in 2010

Throughout the decade John has maintained his passion for weaving and today he is the only commercial pattern weaver working on the Isle of Man. All the mill's knitwear and giftwear is sourced from within the British Isles but cloth is still manufactured in the mill and tradition is maintained where possible. Many modern weavers generate their patterns on computers but John's are designed exclusively by hand. And amazingly, the basic production methods he uses have changed little since the days of the 'cottage' weaver.

The yarn, bought in from Scotland or Yorkshire, arrives into the mill on cones of various colours and shades and these are then placed on the drawer, according to the pattern being worked on. The vertical warp threads are then wound onto the warp mill and thence transferred onto the warper's beam. This is lowered down through trapdoors in the ceiling and placed carefully

A process that has hardly changed in over a hundred years. John Wood operates the warp mill in the Laxey Woollen Mills

John Wood's modern pedal loom

onto a Griffiths pedal loom. The weaver creates a cycling motion which causes the loom to move up and down allowing the horizontal weft threads to interweave with the warp.

One of the main advantages of the hand loom is the ability to stop and start the weaving process at will. Unlike the power looms, which are designed for mass production, the hand loom weaver can adjust his or her pace and take much greater care in the look and feel of the final product. Once John is happy with his cloth it is carefully taken off the loom and he meticulously mends any flaws before it is despatched to a plant in Galashiels for finishing and, if necessary, fringing. The final cloth is then returned to the Laxey mill either for sale by the yard, just as in John Ruskin's day, or made up into gift ware and accessories.

In 2007 John's ability to create his own unique designs led to the production of one hundred limited edition rugs to commemorate the Centenary of the Island's famous TT races. The rugs' design incorporated colours associated with the races – yellow and red flags, black and white flags and the blue, green and red of the number plates. Demand was so great though that the rugs were all sold before the TT even started!

Wool in The Modern World

Today wool is much more than just a sustainable clothing fabric. Astronauts wear it; lofts are insulated with it; nomads make portable homes out of it and babies go to sleep on it. Twenty first century woollen fashion has largely become an amalgamation of previous styles and fabrics, constantly reworked into 'new' concepts. Trends are dictated by the big designers and high street chains change their looks with each season. The downside for British manufacturers is that clothing production is now largely carried out in the East where everything can be done on a vast, and cheaper, scale. Only growing environmental awareness is giving hope to small, local industry as ethical shoppers seek out natural, handmade products with a low 'carbon footprint'.

Happily for wool, it has gained top billing at the forefront of this movement. Despite being around for thousands of years mankind still hasn't managed to entirely emulate its amazing qualities and these are now being recognised by a scheme known as The Wool Project. The scheme, launched by Prince Charles and supported by British farmers, manufacturers, fashion experts and retailers, aims to rebrand wool as a fashionable and eco-friendly fabric for both clothing and home furnishings[1]. As one observer remarked, when compared to other modern fabrics 'wool has the moral high ground'[2]. It's hoped that the project will encourage consumers to appreciate wool's green credentials, sustainability, fire retardant and insulatory properties and thus help farmers by boosting the price of wool worldwide[3].

For tartan the story also continues – but with a twist. In the manner of fashions that go full circle it is touted in fashion magazines as a hot 'new' trend among young designers, appearing on international catwalks in funky blouses, skirts, handbags, scarves and jackets.

> **Did you know?**
> *Wool is used to cover seating in aircraft and trains as it is hard-wearing and has the least fire risk of any textile fibre.*

A New Era

For more than a century woollen cloth produced in Laxey has travelled to all corners of the globe. Thousands of weddings, births and anniversaries have been celebrated with tartan rugs and warm blankets; patriotic dinners and reunions in far continents have seen the proud wearing of 'Manx blue' kilts and ties and the Laxey Manx tartan is now widely recognised as a national emblem. But the story doesn't end there. New life is once again being breathed into the Laxey Woollen Mills. John and Dian have kept the business in the family and in 2007 they began a major refurbishment of the mill and adjoining buildings.

The old office buildings, formerly the willeying sheds, were the first to be revamped retaining many original features and, in tune with John Ruskin's encouragement of art and handicrafts, the former shop and unused workrooms within the mill itself were

The former willeying sheds, now modern offices

Cabinet maker Nigel Thompson at work in Manxbox within Laxey Woollen Mills complex

Where once power looms thundered, the Laxey Woollen Mills now has a new exhibition space

converted into craft units for Manx artisans such as wood workers and artists to produce and sell their work. This concept quickly snowballed into an Island-wide artisan's co-operative called MostlyManx, co-ordinated from the mill. Dozens of talented artisans, from felt makers to blacksmiths, can now showcase their work through shop displays and public exhibitions, and the first floor of the main mill building, where the power looms once thundered, has been converted into a light, modern space for art shows and displays.

The ground floor of the mill, once the spinning and carding floor, has been extensively refurbished, and an embroidery unit and John's working hand loom have been installed alongside the retail displays. Woollen weaving is still at the heart of the mill but, as a 'home' for other craftspeople, it has also become a gathering place where locals and visitors can find creative inspiration and enjoy an alternative day out. Plans for a contemporary tea room, conservatory and landscaped gardens complete the picture of a new mill for a new century.

Egbert Rydings would be proud.

References:
1. The Times Jan 25th 2010, Valerie Elliott
2. The Times Jan 25 2010, Luke Leitch
3. www.princeofwales.gov.uk

APPENDIX ✍

The Language of Wool

The woollen industry has had quite a marked impact on the English language over the centuries, with many expressions and associated words becoming part of our everyday speech.

The tangled web we weave – a complicated life. A piece of woollen cloth is known as a 'web'.

Tying up loose ends – ensuring a job is finished properly. One of the most critical and fiddly jobs for a wool mender was the tying of the loose ends of wool on a finished length of cloth. They used a special knot to prevent it unravelling.

Interwoven – The way in which people or events are criss-crossed, as in the weaving of a fabric.

A common thread – something that holds people together, just as in woven fabric.

To fleece someone – to swindle a gullible victim.

On tenterhooks – keeping someone in suspense. A reference to the tenterhooks from which damp, washed wool was hung to dry and stretch.

To pull the wool over someone's eyes – to hoodwink or blind them to the truth. A reference to the woolly wig of a certain American 19th century lawyer.

Mungo and Jerry – yes, the name of a funky 1970s pop group! but also woollen fabric that might have had recycled rags, cotton or linen used in its manufacture.

Shoddy – an item of inferior quality. In the late nineteenth and early twentieth centuries some woollen manufacturers reprocessed high quality wool items into reusable wool for making into cloth but reprocessed wool is never as strong as pure wool. Shoddy was the best grade of recycled fabric, mungo and jerry were lower down the scale.

Dyed-in-the-wool – Someone who has steadfast, loyal beliefs in a cause or organisation eg. A dyed-in-the-wool Labour supporter. A reference to the colour added to wool before it is processed.

Beavering away – keeping busy. A 'beaver' was a person who processed wool into felt to be used in the hat industry.

In fine fettle – in good, healthy condition. A fettler was employed to clean the machinery in woollen mills of fibres, grease etc. keeping it in good 'fettle'.

Put someone through the mill – give them a tough time or question them rigorously. Young or inexperienced mill workers were often expected to work in every department, 'put through the mill', to learn the trade thoroughly.

Woolly headed – vague or confused. An early 19th century phrase springing from the indistinct, fuzzy outline of wool.

Wild and woolly – an uncivilised, lawless person.

Old Textile Industry Job Titles

Many **old occupations** connected with the woollen industry have long since disappeared but their job titles give a fascinating insight into the range of tasks that had to be undertaken. Many also gave rise to common British surnames.

Alnager or **Ulnager** – An official who examined the quality of woollen goods and stamped them with a seal of approval.

Baler – Person who baled wool.

Bayweaver – Person who wove bay, a fine woollen fabric also known as 'baize'.

Beamer – Person employed in the woollen trade to wind the warp on the roller before putting it on the loom.

Boll – Person who looked after the power looms in the weaving industry.

Bone Picker/Bunter/Rag and Bone Man – Collected rags to be remade into shoddy clothing.

Bowlminder – Person in charge of the vats used for washing raw wool before processing.

Brabener – a weaver. Also Tixter, Textor, Wabster, Webber or Waver.

Bragger – a wool merchant.

Brasiler – a dyer (also Dexter or Litster or Teinter or Tinctor).

Broad cloth weaver – Person who operated a wide loom.

Burler – A quality inspector for woollen clothing.

Burler Mender – A skilled finisher of woven fabrics.

Carder – Operator of a carding machine used to prepare the wool for spinning.

Card Nailer – A person who maintained the teeth (small sharp nails) on the carding machines used for preparing the wool for weaving.

Cloth Dubber – The person who raises the nap of the cloth.

Cloth Lapper – Person who took the wool from the carding machine and made it ready for the next process.

Colour Man – Person who mixed the dyes.

Doubler – The person who operated a machine used to twist together strands of wool.

Draper – Dealer in fabrics, chiefly woollen and linen cloth, readymade clothing and sewing needs.

Drawboy – The weaver's assistant in shawl-making mills. They sat atop the looms and lifted the heavy warps.

'Fear Nothing' Maker – weaver of a thick woollen cloth known as 'fear-nought', used for protective clothing and lining ship's portholes, walls and doors.

Finisher – The person who 'finished' the cloth, making it ready for sale or use.

Fuller (Also Tucker, Walker, Beater) – Person who thickened and cleansed woven cloth by pounding it in water mixed with fuller's earth.

Kempster – A Wool comber.

Logwood grinder – Person who prepared a black dye made from logwood.

Loom tuner – Man who maintained the looms.

Mechanic – Person who uses machinery to produce goods eg. A spinner or weaver.

Outworker - A woollen weaver who worked at home.

Overlooker – Person in charge of the staff in textile mills.

Picker – Person who cast the shuttle on a loom.

Piecer or Billy Piecer – Person, usually a child, who pieced together any threads which broke on the loom.

Reedmaker – Person who made a hand loom weaver's reeds.

Riddler – Person who sorted or classified wool according to its quality.

Roll Turner – A carder of wool into rolls prior to spinning.

Scotch Draper – Person who sold woollen cloth and clothing door-to-door with payment made in instalments.

Scribbler – Person employed in a scribbling mill where the wool was roughly carded before spinning.

Self Acting Minder – Person in charge of the automatic spinning mule.

Shearman – Person who raised the surface of woollen cloth then sheared it to a smooth surface.

Spinster – A woman, usually unmarried, who spun wool for a living.

Stenterer – Person who operated the cloth finishing machine.

Stretcher or Tenter – Person who stretched the fabric onto tenter hooks.

Stripper – Person employed in the woollen trade to remove rubbish from carding machines.

Sweaters – Women who worked for the woollen industry in their own homes, a particularly common practice in 19th century Leeds. Their cramped houses were the original 'sweatshops'.

Tackler – Overlooker of power loom weavers.

Tapicer or Tapiter – Person who wove worsted cloth.

Tozer – Employed to 'toze' or tease wool prior to spinning.

Turning Boy – Young worker who assisted the weaver by turning the bar on the loom.

Warper – Person who set the warp thread onto the looms.

Webster – A female weaver.

Willeyer – Person who throws handfuls of raw wool onto a willeying machine which loosens it and shakes out dirt and foreign matter.

Winder – Person who transferred the yarn from bobbins onto cheeses or into balls ready for weaving.

Wool Driver – Person who took the wool to market.

Wool Factor – A wool merchant's agent.

Wool Man or Wool Stapler – Sorted the wool into different grades.

Wool Comber – Operated machines that separated the fibres ready for spinning.

Manx Wool and Weaving terminology

Arrey – a mill race
Coigee or cogee – a hand loom
Eaddagh – cloth
Eggey – web or piece of cloth
Fess – the spindle of a wheel (Kelly's Dictionary)
Fidder – a weaver
Fidderagh – weaving (or 'of or belonging to a weaver' – Cregeen)
Garmin – a weaver's beam
Gloo – warp, the vertical threads in a woollen cloth
Gorriman or gorrym – wool dyed blue with woad or indigo
Innagh – woof or weft, the horizontal threads in a woollen cloth
Kaart-olley – wool card
Keeir – a naturally dark coloured wool from the English black sheep
Keeir lheeah – cloth made from a blend of undyed black and grey wools
Keeir as gorrym – a blend of 'keeir' and blue-dyed wool
Kialter – rough, unmilled woollen cloth, usually heavy flannel
Lheeah – natural, undyed grey wool
Loaghtan – a dark coloured wool from the native Manx sheep
Mwyllin – mill – a common element in Manx place names, also applied to corn mills
Ollan – wool
Perree bane – a man's coat made of unfinished woollen cloth
Queeyl-sneeuee – spinning wheel
Rollian – spindle whorl (Faragher's Dictionary)
Rollian broachey – bobbin (Faragher's Dictionary)
Snaie – thread
Spaal – a weaver's shuttle
Thie coigee – weaving shed
Thie-yn-Fidder – 'house of the weaver'

Old Manx proverbs

Lhig da'n innagh lhie er y chione s'jerree – 'let the woof lie at the last end' (the woof is the horizontal thread). In other words, always finish your work and do a proper job.
'Bease mraane as bishagey kirree' – 'death of a woman and increase of sheep'. If a farmer's wife died leaving money he could buy more sheep and increase his social standing!
'Goll thie yn ghoayr dy hirrey ollan' – 'going to the goat's house to seek for wool'. Going on a fool's errand.
'Blue, the Manxman's livery' – blue was one of the most popular colours used in early Manx clothing.

(With thanks to Chris Sheard of the Manx Heritage Foundation, Faragher's, Kelly's and Cregeen's Manx Dictionaries)

Photographs and images courtesy of St George's Woollen Mills unless listed otherwise.

Illustrations

Front cover montage Julia Ashby Smyth

Includes photograph of John Ruskin, Elliott and Fry 1869, courtesy of Ruskin Foundation (Ruskin Library, Lancaster University)

Back cover

Photograph of Egbert Rydings courtesy of Manx National Heritage
Photograph of John Wood, courtesy of Bill Petro

Preface

Introduction

Chapter One 1860-80

Chapter Two 1880-1900

Chapter Three 1900-1920

Chapter Four 1920-40

Chapter Five 1940-60

Chapter Six 1960-80

Chapter Seven 1980-2000

Chapter Eight 2000-2010

Selected Bibliography

Brackets indicate the source of the material. In the case of (MNH) this is the Manx National Heritage Library.

Abbreviations:

MNH – Manx National Heritage

MHF – Manx Heritage Foundation

IOMNHAS – Isle of Man Natural History and Antiquarian Society

Published References

The Isle of Man

Belchem, John 'A New History of the Isle of Man Vol. 5' Liverpool University Press 2001

Birch, J.W. 'The Isle of Man – A Study In Economic Geography' Cambridge University Press 1964

British Association Visit to the Isle of Man, IOM Times Sept 17th 1887 (MNH)

Cregneash Guide, Manx Museum and National Trust 1969

Cringle, T. (ed.) 'Here Is the News' The Manx Experience 1992

Gill, W.W 'A Manx Scrapbook No.1' (Chapter 4, Place Lore – Lonan) Arrowsmith 1929

Hall Caine, W.R 'The Isle of Man' Adam & Charles Black 1909

Harrison, S. (ed.) '100 Years of Heritage' MNH 1986

Isle of Man Holiday Guide 1973, The IOM Tourist Board

Jeffcott, J.M 'Manx costume' Presidential Address IOMNHAS delivered 27th March 1890, Yn Lioar Manninagh, Vol.1 pp.153-8

Jenkinson, H. 'Jenkinson's Practical Guide to the Isle of Man', Edward Stanford, London 1874

Kniveton, G. & Goldie, M. 'Tholtans of the Manx Crofter' The Manx Experience, 1986

Kinvig, R.H. 'History of the Isle of Man' Liverpool University Press 1944

Kneen, J.J 'Place Names of the Isle of Man; Part 3 – Garff', Yn Cheshagt Ghailckagh 1926

Kniveton, G. & Scarffe, A. 'The Manx Electric Railway Official Guide – Centenary Year 1993', The Manx Experience 1991

LaMothe, A.E 'Manx Yarns' Manx Sun, 1905 (MNH)

Lewthwaite, Patricia IOM Family History Society Journal Vol.IX No.2 April 1987 (MNH)

McArdle, F. 'Manx Farming and Country Life 1700-1900' MHF 1991

Moore, A.W 'The Surnames and Place Names of the Isle of Man' Elliot Stock, London 1890

Moore, A.W 'A History of the Isle of Man' T.Fisher Unwin, London 1900

Morris, Joseph 'The Isle of Man - Beautiful Britain' Adam & Black, London 1911

Quayle, Elizabeth 'Woman in Mann' IOMNHAS Proceedings No.11 (3) Vol.5 (MNH)

Quayle, Thomas 'General View of Agriculture in the Isle of Man' Bulmer & Co., London, 1812 reproduced by MHF 1992

Quine, Rev. John 'Handbook En Route – Isle of Man Souvenir of Coast and Mountain Electric Railways' IOMT&EP Co., 1899

Quine, Rev. John 'The Isle of Man' reprinted in Cambridge County Geographies F.H.H.Guillemand (ed.), Camb University Press 1911

Robinson, V. & McCarroll, D 'The Isle of Man – Celebrating a Sense of Place' Liverpool University Press 1990

Rydings, Egbert 'Manx Tales', John Heywood, Manchester 1895 (MNH)

Rydings, Egbert Dialect Stories, MS 06213 (MNH)

Shimmin, Ellie 'Life in Ballaugh in the Forties (1840s)' Mannin No.5 p.269

Stenning, Canon E. 'Portrait of the Isle of Man' London, Hale 1975

Train, Joseph 'History of the Isle of Man, Vol.II' M.Quiggin, Douglas 1842

Wilcox, A.G 'Pleasure Island' Cunliffe Bros. 1934

Industry

Bawden, T.A, Garrad, L.S, Qualtrough, J.K, and Scatchard J.W, 'Industrial Archaeology of the Isle of Man' Newton Abbott 1972

Child, John 'Expansion, Trade and Industry' Heinneman 1992

Faragher, Martin 'The Arts and Industry in Victorian Isle of Man' IOMNHAS, April 1995-97 Vol. X No.4, (MNH)

'Manx Industries - The Ruskin Manx Homespuns at Laxey' The Manx Patriot, Vol.1 No.4, Jan 1907 (MNH)

Neff, Wanda F. 'Victorian Working Women – An Historical and Literary Study of Women in British Industries and Professions 1832 – 1850' London, Frank Cass 1966

Raistrick, Arthur 'Industrial Archaeology – An Historical Survey' London, Eyre Methuen 1972

Rosner, David & Markowitz, Gerald.E 'Dying for Work' Indiana University Press 1987

Scarffe, Andrew 'The Great Laxey Mine', MHF, 2004

Speed, P.F 'Social Problems of the Industrial Revolution' Pergamon, 1975

Wohl, Anthony S. 'Endangered Lives – Public Health In Victorian Britain' London, Methuen 1983

Laxey

'An Invitation to Laxey', Official Guide, Laxey Village Commissioners 1960

'Come to Glorious Laxey', Official Guide, Laxey Village Commissioners circa 1970

Bradbury, Dr John 'Our Own Guide to Laxey and its Neighbourhood by a Resident' Tetlow, Stubbs and Company, Oldham, 1876

Boreland, David 'Village Memories of David Boreland – Prominent Laxey Resident from 1879-approx 1965' Ramsey Courier June 22nd 1962, (MNH)

Douglas, Mona 'From Mountain Track to Wearer's Back - A Labour of Love' IOM Times Feb 1st 1963, (MNH)

Kelly, George 'Laxey Businesses and People in the 1920s' Laxey & Lonan Heritage Trust Newsletter No.23 May 2007

Newton, Patricia 'And the Laxey River Runs Down to the Sea' Presidential address IOMNHAS Vol.XII No.1 2005-6 (MNH)

Ordnance Survey Map, Laxey 1869, First Edition, Ordnance Survey Office, Southampton

Rydings, Egbert, Biographical notes and portrait, IOM Victorian Society Newsletter no.47 Aug 1997 p.5 (MNH) L3/VIC

West, Margery 'Peeps into the Past - Ruskin Manx Tweed' IOM Courier, Aug 14th 1970, (MNH)

'The Home of "Ruskin Homespun" Laxey' printed in 'Mercantile Manxland 1900' Representative Business Houses of the Period in the Isle of Man, The Mercantile Reviewing Co. London (p.29) (MNH)

Wool

Allan, D.G.C 'Burials in Woollen 1667 -1814' Journal of Wool Education 1959

Aspin, Christopher 'The Woollen Industry' Shire Publications, 1994

Cowley, J.W. 'The Manx Woollen Industry Through the Ages' lecture to the IOMNHAS, Ramsey Courier 27th Dec. 1957

Hyde, Nina 'The Fabric of History' National Geographic Vol. 173 No.5 May 1988

Howarth, Ralph 'Handloom Weaving in the Isle of Man' 1939 address, IOM NHAS Proceedings V.4 p.360 (MNH)

Quilleash, M. 'Sulby Mill' IOMNHAS Proceedings Vol.VI No.4 1963 (MNH)

St John's Mill information leaflet 2009

Vickers 'The Oiling of Wool' Vickers, Leeds (date unknown)

Vogue Book of British Exports' No.1, Vol.6 Conde Nast Publications, London 1948

Thurston, Violetta 'The Use of Vegetable Dyes' Reckitt & Colman Leisure Ltd. 1977

John Ruskin

Abercrombie Archive, Vol.1, Ruskin Foundation (Ruskin Library, Lancaster University)

Coleing, Linda 'Utility Prefigured: Ruskin and St George's Mill' from 'Utility Reassessed' Manchester University Press 1999

Collingwood, W.G. 'The Life of John Ruskin' Methuen 1893

Cook, Edward T., 'Studies in Ruskin', George Allen, 1890 pp.173-177

Dawson, Margaret 'Ruskin and the Laxey Woollen Industry' 1993 Friends of Ruskin Newsletter, (Brantwood)

Dearden, Dr. James 'John Ruskin – A Life In Pictures' Sheffield Academic Press 1999

Garnett, J.A. 'Honest Trade. John Ruskin's influence on honest manufacture and trade during the late-nineteenth century' (MA dissertation) MS 11503 (MNH)

Priestley, J.B 'Victoria's Heyday' London 1972

Ruskin, John 'General Statement Explaining the Nature and Purposes of St George's Guild' George Allen 1882, Ruskin Foundation (Ruskin Library, Lancaster University)

Ruskin, John 'Fors Clavigera – Letters to the Workingen and Labourers of Great Britain' George Allen, Ruskin Foundation (Ruskin Library, Lancaster University)

Rydings, Egbert 'Some Reminiscences of John Ruskin', The Young Man No.108, July 1895 (Ruskin Foundation, Ruskin Library, Lancaster University)

'St George's Cloth' Pall Mall Gazette, Feb 8th 1886, reprinted in 'The Works of John Ruskin' V.XXX ed. E.T.Cook and A.Wedderburn, George Allen 1907 pp.330-332 Ruskin Foundation (Ruskin Library, Lancaster University)

'The Isle of Man and Textiles – Ruskin Guild Outcome', Manufacturers and Trades Scrapbook, B240 Vol.2. p.175 (MNH)

Sizeranne, R. de la, translated by the Countess of Galloway 'Ruskin and the Religion of Beauty' George Allen, London, 1899

Swan, Alison 'Guild of St George Introductory leaflet', Ruskin Foundation (Ruskin Library, Lancaster University)

Viljoen, Helen (Ed.) 'The Brantwood Diary of John Ruskin' New Haven: Yale University Press, 1971

Unpublished references

Aksoy, Jean 'Study of Agneash' Unpublished Dissertation, Liverpool Hope University 1996

Anderson, Barbara 'The History of the Manx Woollen Industry' 1954. Ref.M677.3 (Douglas Library)

Eagles, Stuart 'Political Ruskin: The Influence of Ruskin's Political Ideas and Social Experiments in Britain circa 1870-1920' Thesis for Doctor of Philosophy Degree, Queen's college Oxford, 2008 Ruskin Foundation (Ruskin Library, Lancaster University)

Howarth, Eric 'Cloth Tentering in the Isle of Man' 1998. Courtesy of Freda Howarth

Newton, Patricia 'Study on the history and architecture of St George's Woollen Mill' 2002

Keggin, Laura 'Industrial Report on Laxey Woollen Mills' Textile Design student 1996

Minutes of a Meeting of St George's Guild, Liverpool, 28th October 1901 Ruskin Foundation (Ruskin Library, Lancaster University)

Rydings, Egbert, Letter to Mr Rudd, 1890 (St George's Woollen Mills)

Rydings, Egbert, Letter to John Ruskin 'Asking to Become a Companion' March 1876 Ruskin Foundation (Ruskin Library, Lancaster University) RF L101

Manx National Heritage Resources (deposited in MNH Library)

Bent's 1902 and 1907 Isle of Man Directory

Brown's 1881/1882 and 1894 Isle of Man Directory, Brown & Sons, IOM Times Office, Douglas

Catalogue of the Isle of Man International Exhibition of Industry, Science and Art 1892 MNH Library B 240/7

Corrin, Daniel, Linen & Woollen Draper, Cloth Hall, Victoria St, Douglas 1888 MNH Library MS5020C

Isle of Man - Laxey Tourist Guides 1950- 1960, Laxey Commissioners, MNH Library MS F78

Isle of Man Official Guide 1947, The Isle of Man Publicity Board

Isle of Man Telephone Directories 1900, 1906, 1928 – 1981

Isle of Man Examiner Annuals

Isle of Man Family History Society Monumental Inscriptions

Lace, Thomas, Weaver of Andreas, Notebook of, MNH Library MS231A

Local Government Board Report (Laxey) July 1891

Lonan Mixed Registers 1849-1883 (106) 184

Mannin No.9, 1917 (letters of T.E. Brown and Egbert Rydings)

Manx Church magazine 1891-92

Manx Quarterly #11 1912 Memorial Notice Egbert Rydings

Manx Year Book 1912 & 1914, Norris-Meyer Press, Douglas

Maps 1867 Sheet X16 Onchan Bowring Mill (woollen)

Mate's Directory 1902 edition, by Rev John Quine, W.Mate & sons 1899

Poor Relief in Lonan – Incumbents Report for 1868 (written c.1890) MNH Library
    F.75

Pigot's Directory 1837

Pigot and Slater's Directory 1843

Porter's 1889 Isle of Man Directory

Report of the Commission of Enquiry on Local Industries 1900, IOM Government
MNH Library B.240

Rydings, Mrs Egbert MMP1121

Rydings, Miss Kathleen MS1272A – 1276A, 5425A, 5426A, MD149,

Smith's Isle of Man Commercial Directory 1883

Thwaites 1863 Isle of Man Directory

Will of Egbert Rydings. MNH Library, 1912. No.158

Newspapers (MNH microfiche)

Manx Advertiser

IoM Times

Manx Sun

IoM Examiner

Manx Star

The Manxman

Isle of Man Census Records
1841 – 51 – 61 – 71 – 81 – 91 – 1901

Useful Web sites

(The author accepts no responsibility for the content of these web sites. Web addresses were correct at time of going to press but may be subject to future changes.)

www.alchemy-works.com for information on dyeing

www.ancestry.co.uk family history

www.bl.uk British Library Newspaper Library

www.brantwood.org.uk Ruskin's Lake District home 1872-1900

www.britishwool.org.uk British Wool Marketing Board

www.edwardianpromenade.com Edwardian fashions

www.essentialvermeer.com for information on dyeing

www.fashion-era.com clothing through the ages

www.isle-of-man.com/manxnotebook Manx history

www.iwias.org.uk Isle of Wight Industrial Archaeology Society

www.iwto.org International Wool Textile Organisation

www.lancashire.gov.uk textile industry history

www.lancs.ac.uk/users/ruskinlib The Ruskin Library, Lancaster University

www.leeds.gov.uk/armleymill textile industry history

www.macclesfield.silk.museum Macclesfield Silk Museum

www.manchester.gov.uk/localstudies textile industry history

www.manchester2002-uk.com textile industry history

www.mers.org.im Manx transport history

www.msim.org.uk Museum of Science and Industry, Manchester

www.nas.gov.uk Scottish family and industrial history

www.nationalarchives.gov.uk family history

www.oldham.gov.uk/localstudies Egbert Rydings

www.on-lineguildwsd.co.uk natural dyeing

www.ozburials.com Herbert Rydings burial record

www.ruskinforall.org.uk The Ruskin Foundation

www.scotlandspeople.com family history

www.scran.co.uk Scottish heritage

www.spinningtheweb.co.uk textile history and facts

www.tartanregister.gov.uk

www.trowbridgemuseum.co.uk/cloth cloth manufacture
www.ukonline.co.uk/thursday.handleigh/demography old occupations
www.welshmills.org.uk woollen mill technical information
www.woad.org.uk for information on dyeing

Index

Acknowledgements

The author would particularly like to thank the archivists and curators of Manx National Heritage, especially the wonderful staff of the Manx Museum Library, for their unstinting help, enthusiasm and encyclopaedic knowledge. Our national archive offers a rich and fascinating resource of Manx life but the people behind it are a resource in themselves – without them this book would have been a mere leaflet. Ditto for Frances Coakley's Manx Notebook – an extraordinary piece of reference work.

Thanks also to Professor Stephen Wildman and staff of the Ruskin Library, Lancaster University; Howard Hull and Sheila Clark at Brantwood, Master of the Guild of St George Dr Jim Dearden and past Guild Secretary Cedric Quayle, Laxey historians Pat Newton and Andrew Scarffe, Brian Roberts at the IoM Public Record Office, Freda Howarth, Robert and Fiona Quayle at Bowring Mill, Peter and Linda Layton, Bill Snelling, Andrew Moore, Heather de Backer and the Manx Guild of Weavers, Spinners & Dyers, Patrick Condon, Paula Harrison and Patricia Haynes for their fine-tooth combing, Jean Aksoy, Head Teacher Laxey School, the British Wool Marketing Board, Oldham Local Studies & Archives, Manchester Local Studies & Archives and the Victoria & Albert Museum Textiles Department.

Special thanks must go to all the Mill employees and Laxey villagers who took the time to share their memories with me; my wonderful supportive family; Julia Ashby Smyth for her inspired, colourful design; Steve at Mannin for his calm reassurance (!) and above all, to Dian and John Wood for entrusting me with such a fascinating story.

Author's Note

I feel incredibly lucky to have been able to read first-hand a wealth of original documentation, mill records, letters and contemporary newspaper articles while researching this book. Most of the leading characters on these pages had strong personalities that still resonate through their hand-writing. The internet proved invaluable for my research but there is nothing like pen, ink and buff-coloured writing paper to make you feel a connection 'across the years'.

This is by no means 'the definitive story' of Laxey weaving – the cottage weavers and mill employees who could have told us what it was really like to work in the industry have sadly left no written records – but it's hoped that what you read here may stir memories or recollections that could help build on a largely unrecorded aspect of Laxey history. Every attempt has been made to maintain factual accuracy but the author accepts full responsibility for any errors or omissions and welcomes any new information that could add to the picture.

There is little doubt, however, that the long history of the Laxey Woollen Mills encapsulates 150 years of change in Manx work practices, social attitudes, tourism and fashion. I'm sure Egbert would have been fascinated.

About the Author

Sue King was born and raised in the Isle of Man but, as a teenager, moved to New Zealand where she gained a degree in English and Social History from Auckland University. Sue enjoyed a successful career in broadcasting before the 'pull of home' brought her back to the Isle of Man. She now lives in Laxey with her husband, the village blacksmith, and young daughter.